Computer Networking:

Beginner's guide for Mastering Computer
Networking and the OSI Model

Introduction

First of all I want to congratulate you and thank you for making the decision to invest in yourself and to become better.

After you'll finish this eBook you'll be able to understand:
- How the Internet works
- How end-devices (such as our smart phones, laptops, tablets) communicate in the Internet
- How does our networks work and of how many types are they
- What is a Router, a Switch, an IP address or a MAC Address
- How can we apply this knowledge in a practical scenario

This book is structured into **8 large chapters** (based on the structure of the OSI model) that will cover various topics that belong to the computer networking world.

I wish you good luck, and if you have any questions, do not hesitate to contact by email, Facebook or YouTube.

If you enjoy this eBook, remember to leave a review HERE and click here to check out my other PRACTICAL guide: **"CCNA Command Guide"** The Complete CCNA Routing & Switching Command Guide for Passing the CCNA Exam

Table of Content

Chapter 7 - Layer 5, 6, 7 - Session, Presentation, Application

Layer 5 - Session

Layer 6 - Presentation

Layer 7 - Application

DHCP

How does DHCP work ?

Configuring an IP address with DHCP on Windows

2) Telnet

3) Secure Shell (SSH)

4) RDP - Remote Desktop Protocol

Chapter 8 - Cisco IOS & Intro to the CLI

Intro to the CLI - Basic Configurations

a) Access Levels

b) Setting a device name (Hostname)

c) Securing access on the Router

d) Configuring an IP address on the Router

f) Configuring remote access on a Router (Telnet, SSH)

Practice Lab + BONUS

Chapter 1 - Basic Networking Elements

A **network** is a group of devices (PCs, Laptops, Servers, smart phones, etc.) **interconnected** that can communicate (exchange information) with each other. All of these devices are interconnected by special network equipment (**Routers** and **Switches**). We'll talk more about Routers and Switches a little bit later, but for now let's see the existing network types.

1) Network Types

Computer networks can be of several types:

*   **LAN** – *Local Area Network* – your home network
*   **MAN** – *Metropolitan Area Network* – extended network, on the surface of a city
*   **WAN** – *Wide Area Network* – multiple networks (LANs) of an organisation interconnected
*   **WWAN** – *World Wide Area Network* – the Internet
*   **WLAN** – *Wireless LAN* – aka Wi-Fi, usually created by our home Router

Also, in addition to these network types, there are other of different sizes or purposes (eg: SAN - Storage Area Network, EPN – Enterprise Private Network, VPN – Virtual Private Network).

Now let's take a closer look at some of the networks discussed above:

A **LAN** is a relatively small network that is **local to an organisation** or a home. For example, your home network is considered a LAN because it is limited in terms of the number of devices connected to it.

A school network (although larger than a home network) is considered a LAN because it interconnects many devices (all computers, servers, etc.) in the same network.

Moving forward to the next network type: if we were to combine multiple networks and allow them to interconnect within a city, then we would form a **MAN** (a much wider network, spread across an entire city that offers *higher transfer speeds* of data than the usual Internet connection).

Now, as I said earlier, a MAN is a network that interconnects multiple networks within a city, the purpose of a **WAN** is to connect the network of multiple cities (or even countries) in order to form a wider network, across a large geographical area. We can also say that *multiple LANs* of an organisation (or multiple organisations) interconnected form a WAN.

A **WLAN** (aka Wi-Fi)is a LAN on which we can connect wirelessly from our smart phones, tablets, laptops or any other device. The wireless environment is separate from the physical (cable) one and has different properties in terms of speed, security, coverage, etc. The main benefit of Wireless connectivity is the flexibility that it offers.

2) Network Components

Now let's move forward and speak a little bit about the components that form a network. So, here they are:

- **End-device** - (PC, Laptop, smart phone, Servers etc.)
- **Switch** - interconnects multiple end-devices within a network (LAN)
- **Router** - interconnects multiple networks (thus forming a WAN)
- **Firewall** - protects our network from potential cyber-attacks from the Internet
- **Transmission medium** – the way we can transmit information (eg: cable or wireless)

Let's take a closer look at the network components listed above:

A. END DEVICE & TRANSMISSION MEDIUM

Generally, we are the ones that have a device (end-device). Each of us has a Laptop, tablet or smart phone with which we connect to the Internet. The connection can be made with 1 or more transmission media (current, light impulses, radio waves).

When we connect with our smart phones to the Internet, we will use the wireless connection. If we use a Laptop or a PC, we can connect it either wirelessly or through a network cable (UTP).

Figure 1.1

We use Fibber optic when we want to connect multiple network or server equipment (ex. switch - switch, server - switch). The reason is simple: a Fibber Optic connection can be much faster than UTP (cable) or Wireless. We can transfer more data (10, 40, 100 Gbps throughput) on a longer range (1 - 5 km or miles).

Also, fibber optics is now being used regularly when connecting a home user to the Internet. The main reason for this is the fact that fibber optics can transfer data at higher speeds and at a longer distance (1 - 5 miles/km) which is way, way more than the classic UTP cable that caps out at 100 meters !

B. SWITCH

A **Switch** (figure 1.2) is a **network device** that *interconnects* multiple end-devices (PCs, laptops, printers, IP phones, Servers etc.) in the same Local Area Network (*LAN*).

It is well known for its **high port density** (generally **24, 48** or even more) capable of speeds between 1 Gbps to 10 Gbps (or even 40 Gbps) per port. The switch uses MAC addresses as a way of identifying the end-devices connected to the network (we will talk in more detail in Chapter 4).

Here is an image with a Cisco **Switch**:

Figure 1.2

C. ROUTER

A **Router** is a network device that has the role of **interconnecting multiple networks** (LANs) thus forming a larger network (**WAN** - Wide Area Network). The Router is the (main) device that **connects us to the Internet**, trough it's ability to handle packet delivery (from any source) to any (destination) network.

The Router achieves this by using **IP addresses** in order to identify the source and the destination devices (we'll talk more about IP addresses in Chapter 3)

When comparing it to a Switch, a Router has way fewer ports (between 2 to 5) at similar speeds (100 Mbps - 10Gbps, depending on the model).

Bellow you can see a Cisco **Router**:

Figure 1.3

3) How can we represent (or "draw") a network ?

Usually networks are being **represented** by a "**network topology**", which can be of 2 types: **logical** or **physical**. Logical topologies describes the logical aspects of a network (the IP addresses of the networks, the way the devices are connected, the routing protocols that are being used, etc.).
The following example is a logical topology and is composed of 2 Routers, 1 PC, and 1 Server. One of the Routers is connected to the Internet

Example # 1 Logical Topology

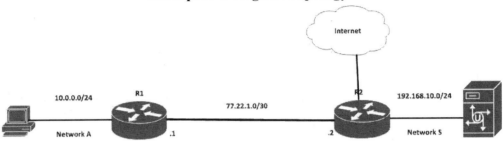

Figure 1.4

In this second example, the network is composed of 1 Switch, 3 Routers, 2 PCs and 1 Server

Example #2 Logical Topology

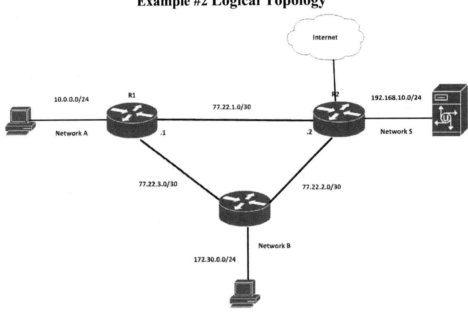

Figure 1.5

Physical topology describes the physical aspect of a network (where are the devices placed, what type of cables are we using, how many ports do we need, on what ports/switch will be the servers connected, etc.) It actually shows where the equipment is (physically) located and it's main purpose within the network.

4) How computers communicate over the Internet ?

In order to communicate (send traffic – aka. connect to Facebook, Google etc), the devices (PCs, Routers, Switches, etc.) must have a **unique identifier**. In the Internet world, this identifier is known as: **IP (Internet Protocol)**.

The IP is the way we identify a device in a network or in the Internet. **It must be unique**. There can't be 2 equal IP addresses in the same network (or in the Internet), because there will be a conflict and the Internet connection will not work properly. Here are 2 examples of an IP address: 192.168.1.170 or 84.222.0.93

```
C:\Windows\system32\cmd.exe

Microsoft Windows [Version 6.1.7601]
Copyright (c) 2009 Microsoft Corporation.  All rights reserved.

C:\Users\oracle>ipconfig

Windows IP Configuration

Ethernet adapter Local Area Connection 2:

   Connection-specific DNS Suffix  . :
   Link-local IPv6 Address . . . . . : fe80::80e7:3223:ac5c:39e9%16
   IPv4 Address. . . . . . . . . . . : 192.168.1.170
   Subnet Mask . . . . . . . . . . . : 255.255.255.0
   Default Gateway . . . . . . . . . : 192.168.1.2

Ethernet adapter Bluetooth Network Connection:

   Media State . . . . . . . . . . . : Media disconnected
   Connection-specific DNS Suffix  . :

Tunnel adapter isatap.{EDB96DF3-34AA-41A1-8809-9B27B2DF11B3}:

   Media State . . . . . . . . . . . : Media disconnected
   Connection-specific DNS Suffix  . :
```

Figure 1.6

In figure 1.6, you can see the command line of Windows (**cmd**). Here's another example of IP address:

10.0.0.1/24, where **/24** is the **network mask**

The **subnet mask** determines the **network size** (ex: how many devices can be connected to the same network at the same time: for /28 there can be no more than 14 devices; for /25 a max of 126; for /24 a max of 254 etc.).

Bellow are the necessary **components** for an end-device to **communicate** (connect) **successfully** in the Internet:

IP address = uniquely identifies a device connected to a network

Network Mask = determines the size of a network (ex: the number of available IP addresses)

Default Gateway = specifies the way out of the network (a Router connected to the Internet)

DNS Server = "transforms" a name (i.e. google.com) into an IP address (i.e. 173.23.85.91)

In the next chapter we are going to talk about the OSI Model which is a framework broken down into 7 layers that explains exactly how the Internet (and communication) works.

Chapter 2 - The OSI Model

The OSI model is a framework that defines the way devices communicate in the Internet (and in our LANs).

This model is divided into **7 layers**, each independent of the other. Thus, changes may occur over time (new protocols, performance improvements, at each layer without interfering with the functionality of the upper (or lower) layer.

The OSI model consists of 7 layers (you can also see the layers in Figure 2.1):

1. **Physical**
2. **Data Link**
3. **Network**
4. **Transport**
5. **Session**
6. **Presentation**
7. **Application**

The OSI model helps us understand (in a more detailed way) how computer networks work and also provides us with a better way of **troubleshooting** (solving problems that may occur in a network, regardless of its size) events that might happen.

Each layer defines how things should operate in the communication process of 2 or more devices. Each layer of the OSI model has it's own protocols that (all combined) define the behaviour of network devices.

For example, when we want to send traffic to a specific server, we need to know where to send that traffic (aka. the destination), so we're going to use the IP protocol (which works at Layer 3 - Network - talk about it more in depth, later). Another scenario could be a request to download a file or access a web page, case in which we're going to use protocols such as FTP or HTTP.

And now, maybe you're asking yourself: "hmm... protocol ? what's a protocol ?" Well.. it's simple:

A *protocol is a set of rules*. That's it ! a set of rules for the way **devices behave** in a network.

As I said at the beginning of this chapter, the majority of the protocols are independent of each other. By designing things this way (thanks to the OSI model), in the case of any changes no other protocols will be affected. In Figure 2.1, below, you can see how the OSI model is structured:

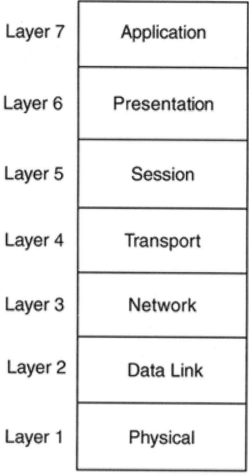

Figure 2.1

As you can see in Figure 2.2, each layer is accompanied (on the left) by a component, called **Protocol Data Unit (PDU)** - or the data units that are being used by each layer:

- Layer 1 uses **Bits**
- Layer 2 uses **Frames**
- Layer 3 uses **Packets**
- Layer 4 uses **Segments** (or **Datagrams**)
- Layer 5 uses **Data**
- Layer 6 uses **Data**
- Layer 7 uses **Data**

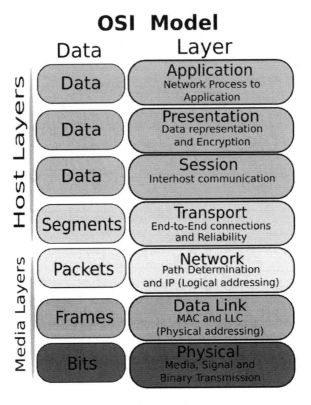

Figure 2.2

In the following chapters we'll talk in much more detail about each layer of the OSI model and you'll get a much clearer understanding of it.

In figure 2.3, you can see a more in-depth example of the OSI model and (briefly) what each of it's layers is all about:

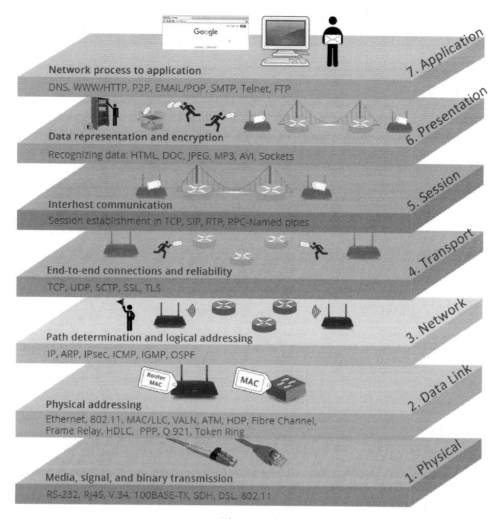

Figure 2.3

For each and every layer you have a very short breakdown of how things work. Don't worry starting with Chapter 3 will dive deep into each and every single one of these layers.

Now, moving forward, I want to tell you that the OSI model is not alone. In "competition" with this model is the **TCP / IP model**, which was created and adopted faster (1974). Currently this model is being used (Figure 2.4). The OSI model was first released in 1984, so there was a clear competitive advantage for the TCP/IP model.

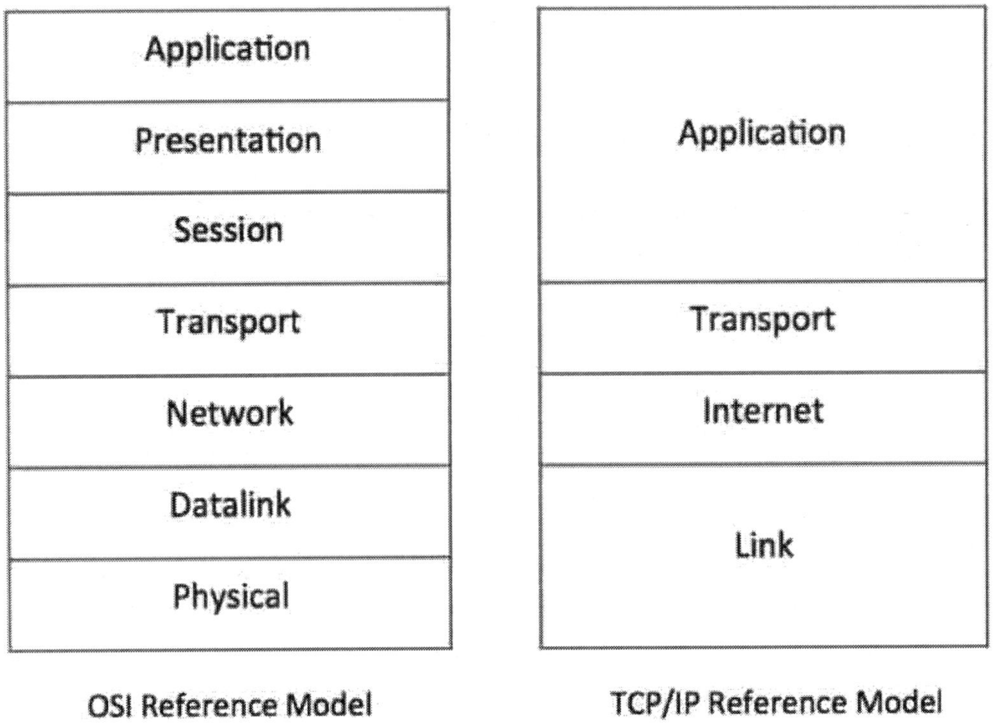

OSI Reference Model	TCP/IP Reference Model
Application	Application
Presentation	
Session	
Transport	Transport
Network	Internet
Datalink	Link
Physical	

OSI Reference Model   TCP/IP Reference Model

Figure 2.4

The TCP / IP model contains only **4 layers** (as opposed to OSI's 7 layer model). At its first layer **includes** the 2 layers (Physical and Data Link) that are part of the OSI model, and the last 3 layers (Application, Presentation and Session) are represented as a single layer in TCP / IP and namely Application. The purpose of these 2 models is to allow communication between 2 or more devices (on which different applications exist).

When a PC wants to send a request for Google's homepage it starts from the Application layer (the request being formatted in many streams of data) and moves down the OSI (or the TCP / IP) model till it reaches the Physical layer (and will be sent - in the format of bits - as electrical signal, light impulses or radio waves down the cable). This process is known as **encapsulation**.

The **reverse** process (ex: when the request reaches Google's web servers - (Physical Layer -> Application) known as **decapsulation**.

Now, let's move forward and start with the first layer of the OSI model, the Physical layer

Chapter 3 - Layer 1 - Physical

So, let's get into the OSI model and start with the 1st of it's layers, the physical layer. When it comes to the **physical layer**, we're going to talk about the medium through which devices send information. The 3 main ways we can connect networks (and devices to networks) are:

1. **Electrical current** (UTP cable with 8 small copper wires)

2. **Light signal** (optical fibber)

3. **Radio waves** (wireless)

The physical layer is at the basis of computer networks because **it provides us with the physical connectivity** between networks (or locations).

Each transmission medium has its own advantages and disadvantages. For **example**: the **advantages of wireless** over cable connection are pretty straightforward: *mobility and flexibility*, while the disadvantages are *lower transfer speeds* and (lack of) *security*.

Instead, a **cable** connection (usually a UTP cable – we'll talk more about it a little bit later) is much more *secure* and *reliable* than **wireless**. It can transport data at **much higher speed** rates (1/10/40 Gbps or more) and can be used over longer distances (up to 80 - 100 m on UTP).

The 2nd way we can transport data is by using light. Here comes the **Fibber Optic** connections (uses light as a signalling method) which allows us to transport data over a longer distance (1 - 5 km or more) than UTP cable (100 m) and at a much higher speed.

UTP Cable Types

Now, let's say that we (you and I) want to connect our laptops together via cable. things might appear very simple. You just take a cable and plug it into my laptop and everything will work just fine, isn't it? Well not so. A **UTP** (Unshielded Twisted Pair) cable contains **8 small wires** (or pins), out of which 4 used for Send and 4 for Receive traffic (and looks as in figure 3.1):

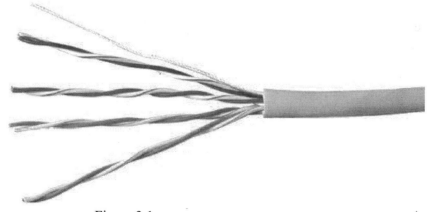

Figure 3.1

Out there are many types of devices (PCs, Laptops, Routers, Switches, Access Points, Firewalls, etc.) and each of them requires a slightly different way of UTP cable (type).

This UTP cable has 2 ends that can be **plugged** in the following ways:
- **Straight** - the wires are the same at both ends
- **Crossover** - the wires are crossed at both ends
- **Rollover** - the wires are rolled over - (used by the console cable)

Each of the devices stated above requires one type of UTP cable when connecting to another one. On the next page you can see how these cable types look like and the required type for multiple devices.

Let's start with the **Straight** cable, which can be used to connect:
- Router <-> Switch
- Switch <-> PC
- Switch <-> Printer (or Server or any other end-device)

Ethernet Straight-through cable T568B

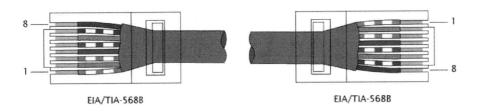

Figure 3.2

And the following devices will use the **Crossover** cable in order to be connected:
- Switch <-> Switch
- Router <-> Router
- Router <-> PC
- PC <-> PC

Ethernet Crossover Cable with RJ45 Connectors

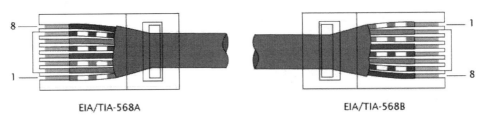

Figure 3.3

As you can see in the examples above (and as a general rule) we can say that the **Straight** cable is used when **connecting different devices** (ex: Router – Switch, Switch – PC, etc.) and the **Crossover** cable is used when **connecting similar devices** (ex: Router – Router, Switch – Switch etc.). An exception to this rule has to do with the Router – PC (or Server) connection.

The Console Cable

Now let's move on and talk about the 3rd UTP cable type, the Rollover cable. When it comes to accessing (via the command line) a Router we have 2 options:

- Connect directly to its **console port**
- **Remote access** via the network (by using **Telnet** or **SSH**)

If we want to connect to the equipment (Router, Switch, etc.) via the console, we need to have **physical access** to the device. In most cases this is not possible. **At first**, when we set up from "0" a brand new network device, we **must connect to it's console port**. The reason being is that we don't have an IP address (on the equipment) to which we can connect remotely.

Also, we must use the console port when we lose access to the device (something happened with the network or with the equipment itself) because then we can investigate the incident (aka. troubleshoot).

In order to connect to any Cisco device through the console we need a special cable, called rollover (see figure 3.4). This type of cable will be inserted in a special port known as the **console port**.

 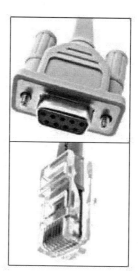

Figure 3.4

In order to **connect** to the Router (or Switch) **directly, via console**, we will also need a special program (such as **PuTTY** - in figure 3.5 below or TeraTerm, SecureCRT, etc.) that will give us access to the command line of the Router (or Switch) - as you can see in figure 3.6.

Figure 3.5

In the figure bellow you can see how the console port (of the Router) is being connected to the laptop on a serial port (or on the Ethernet port by using an adapter):

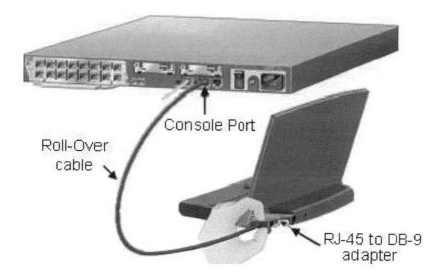

After completing this process, things will look similar to figure 3.6:

```
R1 con0 is now available




Press RETURN to get started.





R1>
R1>
R1>
R1>enable
R1#configure terminal
Enter configuration commands, one per line.  End with CNTL/Z.
R1(config)#exit
R1#
*Mar 20 16:59:10.143: %SYS-5-CONFIG_I: Configured from console by console
R1#
```

Figure 3.6

19

Ports, Interfaces and their speed

A port is the physical way we can connect to the network (basically, it is the **physical part** and is "where the cable plugs in"). An interface is the **"logical" part** of the port (the place we can **set an IP address**).

- In the port we plug the (physical) cable

- On the interface we set the IP address

For each port, the speed may be different. It can vary between 10 Mbps - 100 Gbps (100,000 Mbps), depending on the model and case.

Mbps = Megabits per second

Gbps = Gigabits per second

The current standard in LANs (at the user level) is 1000 Mbps (or 1 Gbps). In Figure 3.7, you can see a Cisco Switch which has 48 Gigabit Ethernet (1000 Mbps) ports and, on the right side, 4 x 10 Gigabit Ethernet ports.

Figure 3.7

It's normal for Switches to have a high port density (52 in this case, but there are other model which have hundreds of ports) because **this device is designed** to connect multiple devices in the same network (LAN).

Full-Duplex / Half-Duplex

Another important element when it comes to how a port works is how data is actually sent.

1. SW1 (and PC A) can send data by turn (the PC sends, the Switch just receives and vice versa: when the Switch sends, the PC receives - this process does **NOT happen simultaneously**) - this mode is known as **Half-Duplex**: Devices can **only** *send* **or** *receive*, but **NOT** at the same time (figure 3.8).

2. SW1 (and PC A) can send and receive data simultaneously - this mode is called **Full-Duplex** and is the one used (figure 3.9).

The benefit of using **Full-Duplex** is clear: faster transfer speeds in the network.

Half-Duplex

Figure 3.8

Full-Duplex

Figure 3.9

Collision domains and Broadcast domains

In any network, a packet can reach different points in the network or conflict with other packets transmitted simultaneously: here we'll be talking about the broadcast and collision domains.

1) Collision domains

A **collision** refers to the fact that two different devices send a packet in the network at the same time. If the two packets are sent simultaneously, then a collision is formed. The reason being the way network devices and PCs used to work at the beginning of the Internet (when technology was not as advanced as today).

In the early days of the Internet ('80s - '90s) devices where operating in the half-duplex mode - a single device in the network was sending traffic at a given time, while the other devices connected to the same network had to wait for the first one to finish, in order to be able to send any traffic.

This was the way the networks operated in the 1990s and early 2000s. The collision-solving mechanism was called CSMA / CD (Carrier Sense Multi Access with Collision Detection).

A **collision** can only take place on a **segment** (the connection between two devices: Switch - PC, PC - PC, Switch - Router, etc.) **half - duplex** from a network. Such collisions do not take place (or occur very rarely due to errors) because each device transmits the traffic in **full-duplex** mode.

2) Broadcast domains

A broadcast domain is the distance a packet (of type broadcast) can travel over the network. In other words, how far a broadcast packet can reach within a network will represent the broadcast domain.

In figure 3.11 you might wonder: "*why the connection between Routers is a broadcast domain? Isn't that a collision domain ?*"

The answer is yes and yes. :) It's a broadcast domain because every **interface of a Router represents a new network** and is a collision domain because it is a network segment and as we said earlier: a collision can take place on any network segment (usually half-duplex).

In the images below (Figure 3.10 and 3.11) you can see the collision domains, respectively the broadcast domains of a network topology. As you can see in Figure 3.10 there are **4 collision domains**:

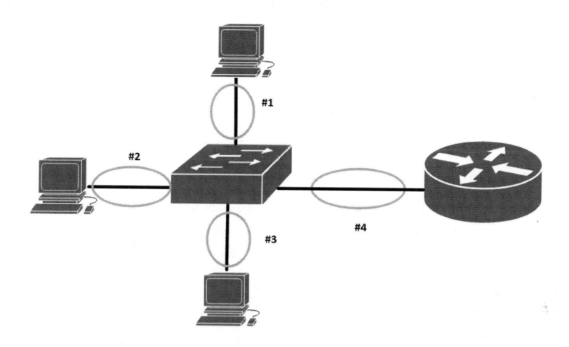

Figure 3.10

And in figure 3.10 there are **4 broadcast domains**:

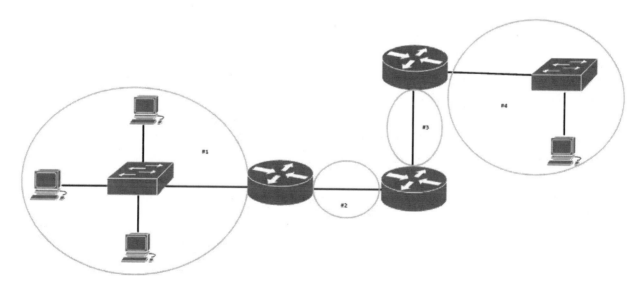

Figure 3.11

Chapter 4 - Layer 2 - Data-Link

Basic Switching concepts

Moving forward to the 2nd layer of the OSI model, let's talk about Switches. So, what is a Switch ? **A switch** is a network device running at **the 2nd layer of the OSI model**. Its **purpose** is to **interconnect** multiple devices (PCs, Laptops, Servers, Printers, etc.) into the **same** local area network (**LAN**). The Switch can do this because it contains multiple **ports (24** or **48** depending on the model) that allows other devices to connect to it via a UTP cable.

Figure 4.1

The vast majority of today's Switches use the **Ethernet technology**. One of the reason of Ethernet's wide spread (and adoption) is its **superior data transfer speed/bandwidth** (1 Gbps / 10 Gbps / 40 Gbps or even 100 Gbps) compared to other existing technologies (Token Ring, FDDI, etc.) that were available when Ethernet first came out.

Ethernet is extremely useful because it lets the Switch know where to send data from one device to another (**based on the MAC addresses** - source and destination). A **MAC address** is a **unique identifier** for each device connected to a network. This address is **written on the NIC** (Network Interface Card) of every single device, by the vendor that manufactures it (ex: Intel, Broadcom, TP-Link etc.).

In figure 4.2 you will be able to see a representation of the MAC address from the command line of Windows. You can find your MAC address by clicking "**Start**" -> (type) **cmd** -> (then type the command) "**ipconfig /all**"

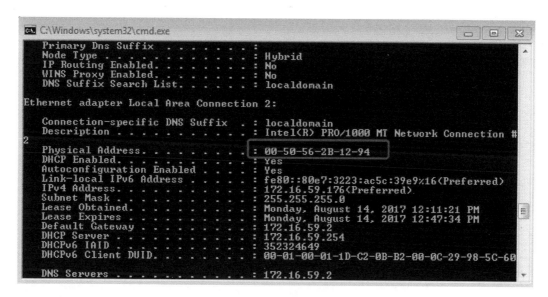

Figure 4.2

The MAC address from figure 4.2 is 00-50-56-2B-12-94 and is represented in hexadecimal format, **48 bits** (12 characters, 4 bits per character). The **first 24 bits** (00-50-56) represent the "**vendor** ID" (ex. Cisco, Apple, Intel etc.), and the next 24 bits (2B-12-94) represents the **device-specific part** that uniquely identifies a device in a network.

What is Ethernet ?

I'm pretty sure that you've heard about Ethernet before. Why ? Because...

1. I reminded it a little earlier :D and...
2. because your home Router uses this technology (just like your PC or Laptop) - take a look at the NIC - network interface

Today, **Ethernet**, is the most widespread network technology, mainly due to the following characteristics:

- **Higher transfer speeds** (10/40/100 Gigabit per second)

- **The Way of identifying** (addressing) **devices** (**MAC** addresses) in a network

25

Today's Routers and Switches all use the Ethernet standard (on their ports). These ports can be **labelled** by using one of the following speed rates:

- **FastEthernet** - 100Mbps (aka. Fa0/1 ... Fa0/24)

- **GigabitEthernet** - 1000Mbps (aka. Gi0/1 ... Gi0/24)

- **TenGigabitEthernet** - 10000Mbps (aka. TenGi0/1 ... TenGi0/24)

Thus, as the devices send traffic to the network, **the Switch will learn their source (MAC)** address and **associate** them with the **ports** they come from (the port on which the device is connected - ex: Fa0/1, Fa0/10 or Gi0/4 etc.)

In figure 4.3, you can see how the **Ethernet header** looks like:

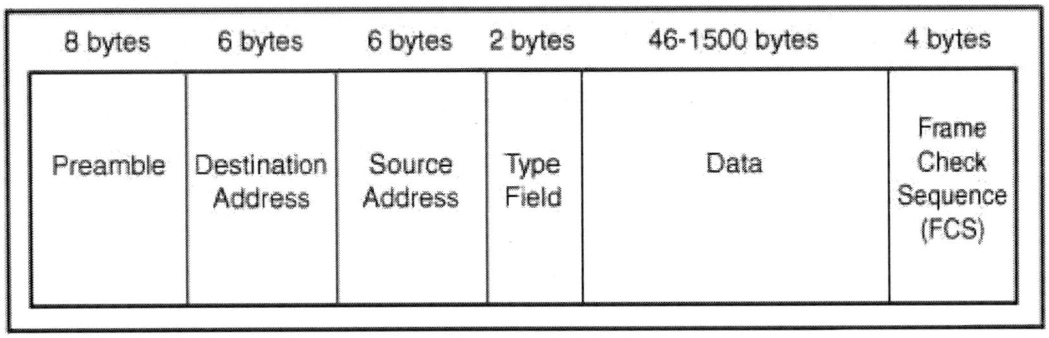

8 bytes	6 bytes	6 bytes	2 bytes	46-1500 bytes	4 bytes
Preamble	Destination Address	Source Address	Type Field	Data	Frame Check Sequence (FCS)

Figure 4.3

Let's talk a little bit more in detail about each component of the Ethernet header:

1. **Preamble -** a string of bits that indicates the beginning of a frame

2. **Destination Address -** the destination MAC address

3. **Source Address -** the source MAC address

4. **Type Field -** Indicates the Ethernet version being used and the length of the frame

5. **Data -** represents the actual transmitted data (together with the upper layer headers)

6. **FCS -** way of checking the integrity of the frame (frame sent = frame received)

7. **EoF** (End of Frame bits) - series of special bits indicating the frame termination (not in figure)

Now, let's see how the Ethernet header really looks in a Wireshark packet capture (figure 4.4):

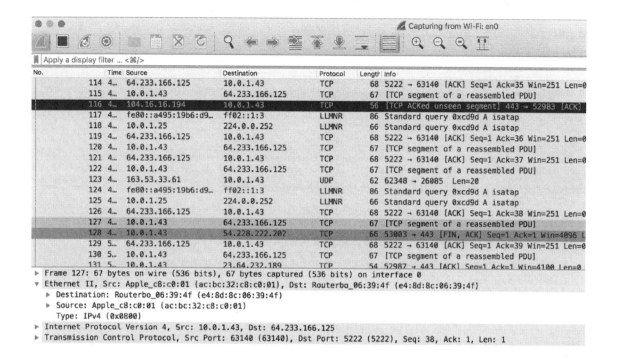

Figure 4.4

Wireshark is a cool tool. It's a program that let's us see the network traffic that is being generated by our machine (laptop, PC, server etc.). In Figure 4.4 you can see how the communication between our device and other devices from the Internet (or LAN) works. Although at first it can be overwhelming, bear with me because we are going to focus only on 1 packet (or data stream).

As you can see I've selected (grey line) a random data stream that allows us to see even deeper into the packet. Here's what we can identify from the lower part of the image:

- TCP data stream between 2 devices (more about it in chapter 6)
- IP addresses (more about it in chapter 5)
- **Ethernet II**, where you can easily identify the **2 MAC addresses** (destination and source).

Now that we've talked about Ethernet, let's move on and talk about how Switches and the switching process work.

oes the Switch learns and uses MAC addresses ?

ose of a **Switch is to interconnect multiple devices** in the same network (LAN). He does ing **MAC addresses** (source and destination).

tination MAC address is being used to identify and send traffic to a device from the network (aka. The destination), while the **source MAC** address is used to **store the port** on which a device is located.

So practically, the Switch **learns** about each device in the network based on its **source MAC address** and decides where to send it based on the *destination MAC address.*

The **Switch keeps** all of this information in a special memory known as the **CAM** (Content-Addressable Memory) table. This **CAM table** describes what the MAC address (source) is on a port (in other words, makes a port mapping / association MAC address - example: The MAC address X is on the Fa0 / 5 port, MAC address G is on port Fa0 / 9.

Let's take the topology network of Figure 4.5 in which 3 PCs are linked to a Switch:

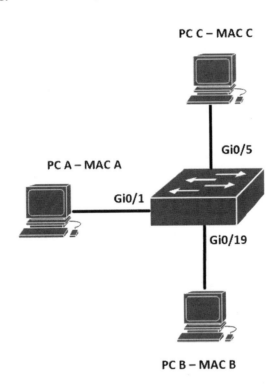

Figure 4.5

28

Basically, the CAM table of the Switch from Figure 4.5 will look (in the beginning) like this:

ID	MAC Addresses	Port
1		Gi0/1
2		Gi0/19
3		Gi0/5

Table 4.1

As you can see in table 4.1, in the beginning (immediately after boot) the **CAM table is empty**. In other words, **the Switch doesn't know the MAC addresses** of the connected devices.

Now let's imagine that the 3 PCs from figure 4.5 are starting to communicate over the network. How are they doing it ? What's going to happen with the Switch ? What is he going to do ?

In the following steps (1 - 5) and tables you'll be able to see how the Switching process works. So let's see:

1) PC A sends the message to PC B

The **Switch** will **learn PC A's MAC** address on port Gi0/1.

ID	MAC Addresses	Port
1	A	Gi0/1
2		Gi0/19
3		Gi0/5

The Switch **sends the message** as a **broadcast** because he doesn't know on which port PC B is connected.

2) PC B receives the message

ID	MAC Addresses	Port
1	A	Gi0/1
2		Gi0/19
3		Gi0/5

3) PC B replies to PC A

The Switch learns the MAC address of PC B and sends the message (based on his CAM table) to PC A on port Gi0/1.

ID	MAC Addresses	Port
1	A	Gi0/1
2	B	Gi0/19
3		Gi0/5

4) PC B sends a message to PC C

The Switch **sends the message** as a **broadcast** because he doesn't know on which port PC C (MAC address) is.

ID	MAC Addresses	Port
1	A	Gi0/1
2	B	Gi0/19
3		Gi0/5

5) PC C replies to PC B

The Switch learns the MAC address of PC C and sends the message (based on its CAM table) to PC B.

ID	MAC Addresses	Port
1	A	Gi0/1
2	B	Gi0/19
3	C	Gi0/5

Now in this stage, the Switch knows every single MAC address from the network. If any other devices would join the network, the **process** will **repeat** for any **unknown** (by the Switch) MAC address.
If any devices stops sending traffic for more than 300 seconds (**5 minutes**) the Switch will **flush** it's MAC address from the CAM table.

Besides the Ethernet standard, there are other standards/protocols that work at **the 2nd layer of the OSI model** (I'm just going to mention them):
- **PPP** (Point-to-Point Protocol)
- **PPPoE** (Point-to-Point Protocol over Ethernet) - used by ISPs for its authentication feature
- **MPLS** - the current protocol/standard for organizations to connect their sites via the ISP
- **Frame Relay / ATM** - older technologies (not being used anymore)

*ISP = Internet Service Provider

Chapter 5 - Layer 3 - Network

Basic Routing concepts

As you saw, the **MAC** address is **only used** for communication within the local network. For example it is used when 2 PCs send traffic between each other in the LAN. If they try to communicate in the Internet, then an **IP address** (and a Router) is required.

The purpose of a **Router** (figure 5.1 - Cisco 2811 model) is to **connect multiple networks** (eg: LAN) into a larger network (often called a WAN - Wide Area Network). Thus the Router's main purpose is to make a simple decision for every single packet that comes in:

"On what interface should I send this packet? And if I don't know where to send it I'll drop it. "

Figure 5.1

By knowing multiple network's location a Router can send the traffic from one network to the other. This process of moving the traffic forward towards its destinations is known as **routing**.

ATTENTION! By default, a **Router** only **knows its Directly Connected** networks. He does not know how to send packets further from them. This is where we, the administrators, come in. We'll have to tell the Router on which way to go in order to reach the destination

When a Router boots up, he **first learns** about his **directly connected networks** (those starting with C in Figure 5.2). In the figure 5.2, you can see the routing table of a Cisco Router, which contains the directly connected networks (C) and the IP address of R1 on those interfaces (L).

```
R1
R1#
R1#
R1#
R1#sh
R1#show ip ro
R1#show ip route
Codes: L - local, C - connected, S - static, R - RIP, M - mobile, B - BGP
       D - EIGRP, EX - EIGRP external, O - OSPF, IA - OSPF inter area
       N1 - OSPF NSSA external type 1, N2 - OSPF NSSA external type 2
       E1 - OSPF external type 1, E2 - OSPF external type 2
       i - IS-IS, su - IS-IS summary, L1 - IS-IS level-1, L2 - IS-IS level-2
       ia - IS-IS inter area, * - candidate default, U - per-user static route
       o - ODR, P - periodic downloaded static route, H - NHRP, l - LISP
       + - replicated route, % - next hop override

Gateway of last resort is not set

      10.0.0.0/8 is variably subnetted, 2 subnets, 2 masks
C        10.0.0.0/24 is directly connected, GigabitEthernet2/0
L        10.0.0.1/32 is directly connected, GigabitEthernet2/0
      77.0.0.0/8 is variably subnetted, 2 subnets, 2 masks
C        77.22.1.0/30 is directly connected, GigabitEthernet1/0
L        77.22.1.1/32 is directly connected, GigabitEthernet1/0
R1#
```

Figure 5.2

To make the routing process possible, the Router uses the **destination IP address** as a reference point (*"to whom should the traffic be sent ?"* - the **destination**) and the source IP address as *"from where did the traffic came from ?"* (the **source**).

In order to send the traffic (packets) to its destination, the Router needs to know, first of all, the destination. This can be done only if the **Router learns** how to reach that destination, process that can be achieved by one of 2 ways:

- **Manual** - via Static Routes

- **Dynamic** - via Routing Protocols (RIP, OSPF, EIGRP)

In the following sections we will start talking about the **IPv4** and **IPv6** protocols (and addresses), then in Chapter 8, we'll move on to the practical side and configure a Cisco Router in the network simulator, Cisco Packet Tracer.

So #1… what is IPv4 ?

The **IPv4 protocol** was developed in the 1980s and it was designed to use **32 bits** of data in order to define an IP address (ex: **192.168.1.1**). As you can see in the example 192.168.1.1, there are 4 fields separated by dots and each field of these 4 can be allocated 8 bits of data:

8 bits * **4** fields = **32** bits.

Now let's think a bit about this number of bits, 32. It can tell us something about the maximum number of IP addresses that can be generated: $2 \wedge 32 \sim= $ **4.3 Billion**! Yeah, you read it well, 4.3 billion IPv4 addresses ... and the are **all allocated**.

TIP: why $2 \wedge 32$? because each bit can be 0 or 1, so if we have 32 bits we can generate about 4.3 billion unique numbers/addresses.

In 2011, exactly in the summer of that year, **IANA** (Internet Assigned Numbers Authority) has allocated the last IPv4 address space. Does that mean we can't connect other devices to the Internet anymore? Not at all. Since then, the Internet has grown a lot. Here's a graph (figure 5.3) which predicts the growth of the Internet in terms of the connected devices:

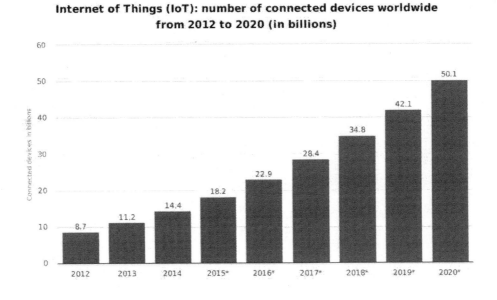

Figure 5.3

NOTE: please note that there is a difference between being allocated and being used. IANA has provided all of it's available IP addresses to the Service Providers (ISP) from around the world, but these addresses are far from being USED by the ISP (or more exactly used by us, the consumers)

As I said earlier, the maximum number of IPv4 addresses is **~4.3 Billion**.

In 2016, it was estimated that the **total number** of **devices connected** to the **Internet** is around **~20 billion**, which by far exceeds the IPv4 address number.

Due to this problem, measures have been taken to **slow IPv4 addressing** allocation by using techniques such as NAT (and also to introduce the concept of *Public and Private IP*). To another extent, far better than NAT is the introduction of the **IPv6 protocol**, which we will discuss a little bit later.

The Structure of an IPv4 Packet

In figure 5.4 you can see the structure (header) of an IPv4 packet

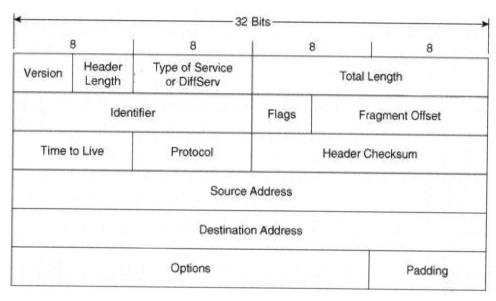

Figure 5.4

Here we can identify some important components that we'll interact with in many situations throughout our IT studies/career:

- **IP Source Address**

- **IP Destination Address**

- **TTL (Time to Live)**

- **ToS (Type of Service)**

- **Header Checksum**

Now let's talk about each of these in more detail and we'll start with the IP addresses. I assume that it's clear the fact that in any communication, between 2 devices, we need a *source address* and a *destination*   *address.*

In this case, the two fields (Source & Destination Address) are reserved for the **source IP** address and **destination IP** address.

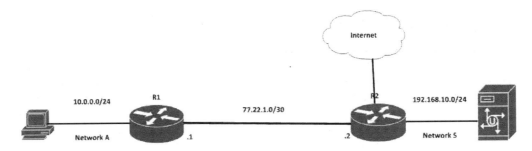

Figure 5.5

For example, in Figure 5.5 you can see the 2 networks: A and S. If the PC from Network A (with the IP 10.0.0.5) wants to communicate with the server (with the IP 192.168.10.8) from network S, then the source address of each packet will be **10.0.0.5** (PC's IP), and the destination address will be **192.168.10.8** (Server's IP).

IPv4 Classes

As I said at the beginning of this chapter, each field (4 in total) of an IP address can have any value between **0 - 255** (8 bits / field, so 256 values, 2 ^ 8 = 256). Thus, IP addresses are divided into several classes:

IP Class	Start IP	End IP	Network Prefix
A	1.0.0.0	127.255.255.255	1 - 127
B	128.0.0.0	191.255.255.255	128 - 191
C	192.0.0.0	223.255.255.255	192 - 223
D	224.0.0.0	239.255.255.255	224 - 239
E	240.0.0.0	255.255.255.255	240 - 255

Classes A, B and C are the ones **used in the Internet**, Class D being reserved for Multicast addresses and Class E is an experimental class that is not being used.

Public IP vs Private IP

Public IP addresses, as their name says, are used to communicate (transit) over the (Public) Internet and the **Private IP** addresses are used in Local Area Networks (**LANs**), such as our home's network or our school's network.

Thus, **Private IP addresses will never reach the Internet**. In order for us to be able to communicate over the Internet, a protocol such as **NAT** (Network Address Translation) was created with the purpose of *transforming Private IPs into Public IPs*.

Private IP Addresses

In the table below are the ranges of the Private IP addresses out there:

IP Class	Start IP	IP End	Network Prefix
A	10.0.0.1	10.255.255.255	10.0.0.0/8
B	172.16.0.1	172.31.255.255	172.16.0.0/12
C	192.168.0.1	192.168.255.255	192.168.0.0/16

NOTE: The rest of the IP addresses not mentioned in this table are PUBLIC !

Thus, we can have a scenario similar to the one in figure 5.4 below (multiple LANs - Network A and S - which contain private IP addressing and public IP addressing for the rest of the networks).

Also, these Private IP addresses (with the help of NAT) improves our **network's security** making it harder for potential attackers to enter it.

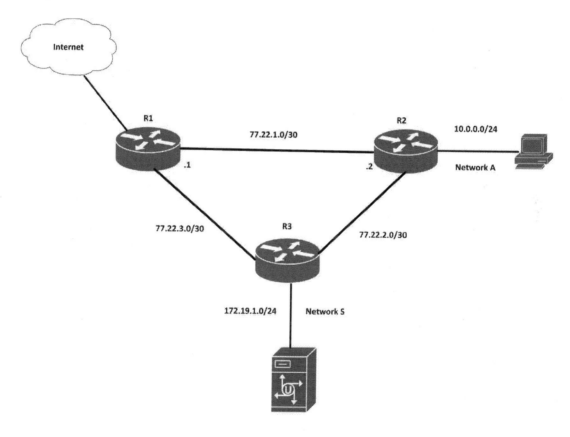

Figure 5.6

37

3 ways of sending Packets in the Network

Have you ever thought of how does end-devices or network devices send the packets in the network ? Well, here are the 3 options available out there:

- *Unicast*
- *Multicast*
- *Broadcast*

In **Unicast mode**, communication between 2 devices is **1 to 1**. That means there is a single source and a single destination. Think of unicast as talking to a friend (you're addressing to a single person).

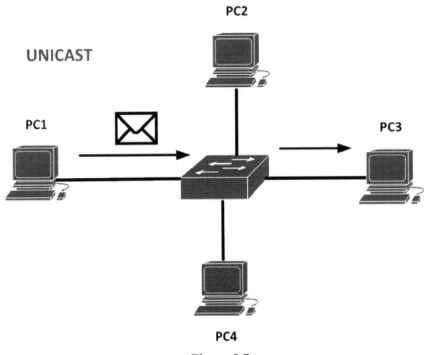

Figure 5.7

In **Multicast mode**, the communication between devices is **1 to g** (specific group of devices). Imagine that you are in a room with 100 people, and you only have a conversation with a group of 10 people / colleagues (aka specific group). That is multicast.

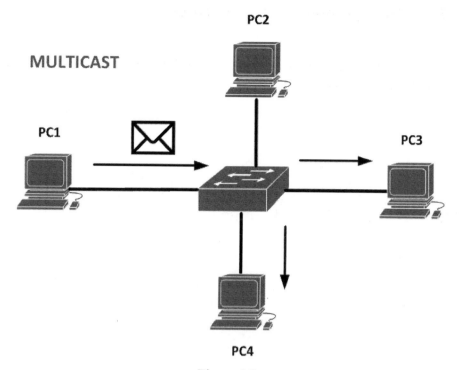

Figure 5.8

In **Broadcast mode**, the communication between devices is **1 to n** (where n represents all devices in the network). **The Broadcast traffic is intended for every device in the network**.

Once again, imagine you are in the same room with 100 people, you are on a stage and you talk to everyone. This is the equivalent of the broadcast.

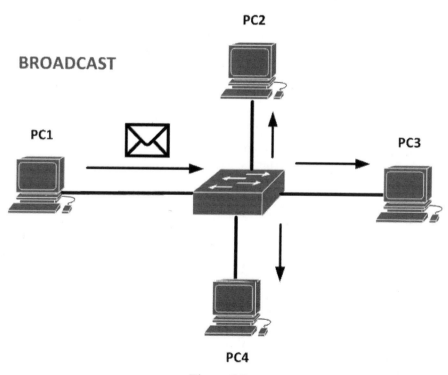

Figure 5.9

Configuring an IP address on Windows 7/8/10

On Windows, when it comes to setting up an IP address, we have 2 options (from the command line or from the GUI). First we'll start by checking our IP address from the command line:

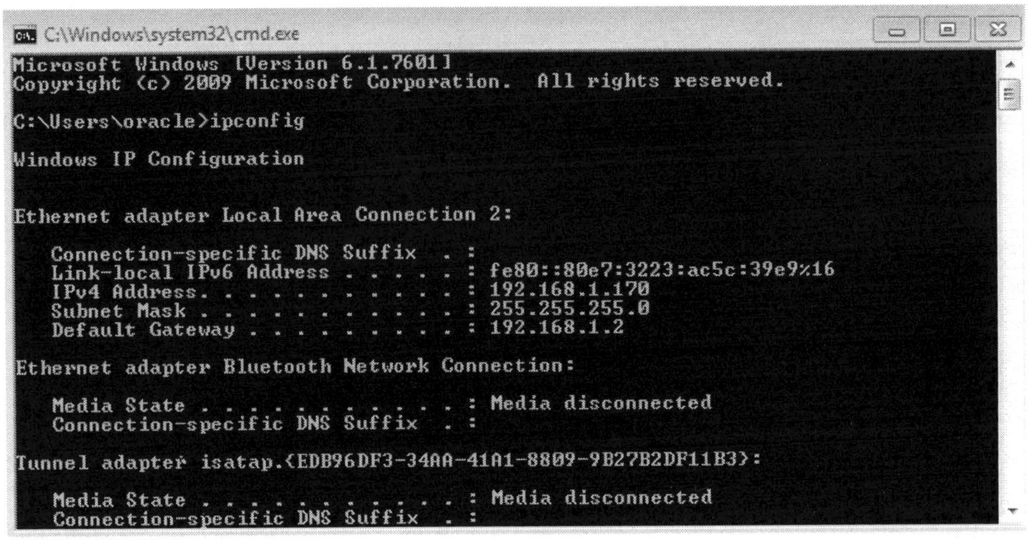

Figure 5.10

The command that's used in figure 5.10 is >**ipconfig** and as you can see, it shows us more information about the Ethernet (LAN), Wi-Fi, Bluetooth adapters. The most important elements shown by the command's output are:

- *IPv4 Address*
- *Network Mask*
- *Default gateway*
- *IPv6 Address*

All of these elements can be configured in one of 2 ways:
- **Statically** - we'll assign all of the info manually
- **Dynamically** - a protocol (such as DHCP) was configured on a server and assign dynamically IP addresses with no human interaction at all.

Ok, now let's see how can we configure in Windows 7 (8.1 or 10) all of the elements mentioned above. In figures 5.11 and 5.12, you'll be able to see how can we do this:

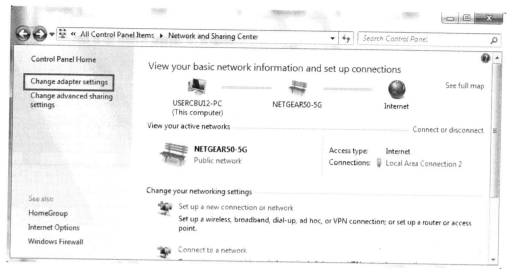

Figure 5.11

A very simple way to configure a **static IP address** is to go to the "**Control Panel -> Network and Sharing Center**" first, followed by "**Change adapter settings**" (or **Network and Internet -> Network Connections**). Now you'll reach a window similar to the one shown in the figure 5.12:

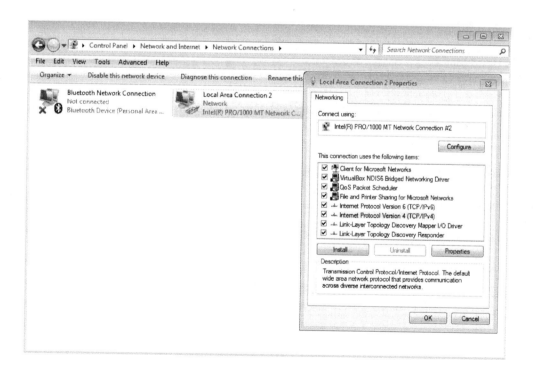

Figure 5.12

Here, we are looking for the "**Local Area Connection 2**" (in your case might be a similar name), and **right click** on it, followed by **"Properties"**. A new window will open, from which we'll **select IPv4** and then **click on Properties**.

At this point we have reached a similar windows to the one in figure 5.13. Here we can (finally) set *the IP address, the Subnet Mask, Default Gateway and the DNS Server*:

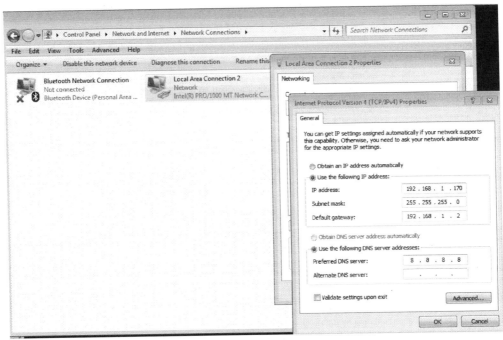

Figure 5.13

Now let's choose, for the sake of the example, a network from which we'll select the other elements required to have access to the Internet. The network's IP address will be 192.168.1.0/24, out of which **192.168.1.170** will be assigned to the PC (Windows 7). The **/24** in decimal mask looks 255.255.255.0 and the **default gateway** (the Internet-connected Router) will have the IP address of 192.168.1.2.

We also need to set the **DNS** server (the one that helps us with the name resolution: from a domain (ex: google.com) will provide us with its IP address (ex: 216.58.214.227)) with the IP address of **8.8.8.8**

Now that we're done with all of these settings, we can check our configuration (from CMD) using the following commands:
>**ping 8.8.8.8**   //checks the Internet connection(actually to 8.8.8.8, which is Google's server)
>**ping google.ro**   //checks the DNS service **and** the Internet connection
>**nslookup google.ro**   //checks the DNS service

In the next section we'll start talking about the successor of IPv4, the "new" **IPv6** protocol.

So #2... What is IPv6 ?

Today, there are more than 20 Billion devices connected to the Internet all around the world and the number just gets bigger and bigger as day pass by. This is a major problem especially for ISPs (Internet Service Providers) because it exceeds by far the number of 4.3 Billion which IPv4 was providing.

So here comes the need for a better, much larger protocol which is known as IPv6. IPv6 is a new addressing (identification) protocol that introduces a new address format (in hexadecimal) and much, **much larger addressing space**, has emerged.

IPv6 is 128 bits long (that means we have **2 ^ 128** addresses available), which is an infinitely larger space compared to IPv4 (that is only 32 bits long). Besides these features IPv6 has many other and will streamline the communication process of devices in the Internet making it more faster and more secure. According to Wikipedia, this number looks like:

"340,282,366,920,938,463,463,374,607,431,768,211,456   or **$3.4×10^{38}$** (340 trillions of trillions of trillions)"

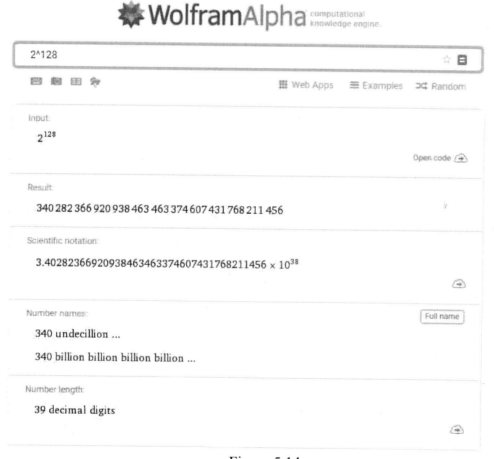

Figure 5.14

Here are a few examples of IPv6 addresses:

- **2001:DB8:85A3:8D45:119:8C2A:370:734B /64**
- **FE80::C001:37FF:FE6C:0/64**
- **2001::1/128**

As you can see, IPv6 addresses are represented in the **hexadecimal format** (it includes **digits 0-9** and **letters A-F**). An IPv6 address is comprised of up to **8 fields** and a network mask (indicating how large the network is - the number of addresses).

Notes: Each IPv6 address field is separated by ":", but there can be a few exceptions:

2002:ABCD:1234:BBBA:0000:0000:0000:0001/64 can also be written in the following ways:

a) 2002:ABCD:1234:BBBA:**0:0:0:**1/64

b) 2002:ABCD:1234:BBBA::1/64

If we want to **reduce** a whole **integer of 0s**, we will simplify it by ":::". **ATTENTION** ! ":::" can be **used** only **once**.

In Figure 5.15 below, you can see an IPv6 address (command >**ipconfig**) from CMD that begins with the notation of **FE80**:...

This **IPv6 address** is a **special** one, in the sense that it can only be used in the local area network (**LAN**) to communicate with other devices.

This types of addresses are known as **Local Link** and are generated automatically (another important feature of IPv6 - address auto-configuration).

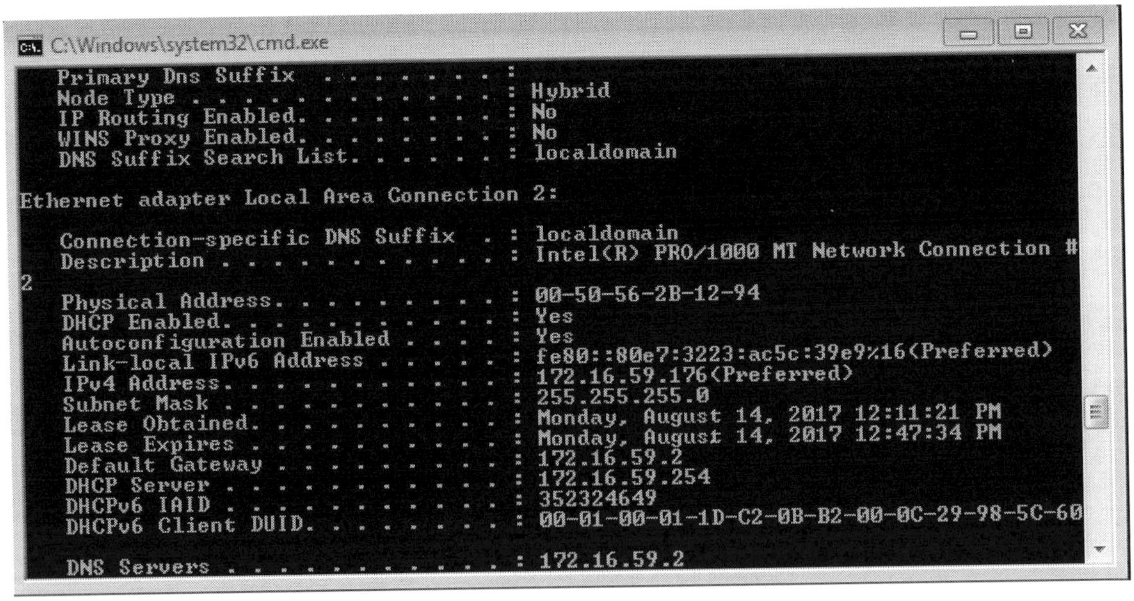

Figure 5.15

Chapter 6 - Layer 4 - Transport

TCP, UDP and Ports

1) TCP

TCP comes from **Transmission Control Protocol** and it does exactly what it says: ensures the transmission control of every single packet within a communication channel.

It can be found (together with UDP) at the 4th layer of the OSI model, the Transport layer. As a PDU (Protocol Data Unit), **TCP uses segments** (it brakes the data into smaller pieces known as segments).

TCP is a protocol that's being used (by you, me and everyone else in the Internet) all the time (without being aware of it). That's because it does a great job in keeping this seamless.

For example, when we download a file from the Internet, or access a web page or **connect in any way to a network device**, we use the TCP protocol.

Now comes the question: **Why? Why do we need it?** Because TCP allows us to communicate by sharing the exact data (ex: web page) that the server or the client has. So when we download a file (through FTP), TCP will ensure that **each segment** composing the file (that's located on the server) will be received and in case of missing segments, to be retransmitted.

So here are some of the features and benefits of the TCP protocol:
*   **Retransmission** of data (in case it's being "lost on the road")
*   **Packet reordering**
*   **Establishes a connection** between the client and the server (3-way handshake)

TCP achieves the elements mentioned above by using the following message types:
*   **SYN, ACK, FIN**
*   **PSH, RST, URG**

We'll talk more about them in the following sections. Now let's move on to the next page and see how TCP works. In figure 6.1 you can see the **TCP header structure:**

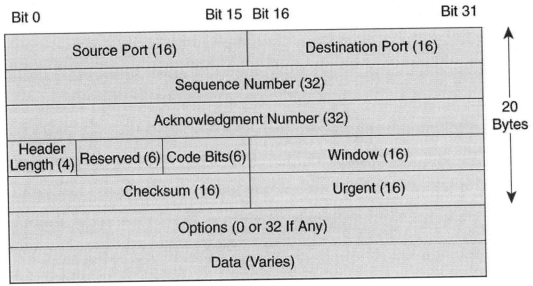

Figure 6.1

And in figure 6.2 you can see it in a **Wireshark capture:**

```
▷ Ethernet II, Src: IntelCor_22:69:1f (e4:a7:a0:22:69:1f), Dst: All-HSRP-routers_50 (00:00:0c:07:ac:50)
▷ Internet Protocol Version 4, Src: 10.84.166.102, Dst: 10.92.32.10
◢ Transmission Control Protocol, Src Port: 64806 (64806), Dst Port: 80 (80), Seq: 0, Len: 0
     Source Port: 64806
     Destination Port: 80
     [Stream index: 109]
     [TCP Segment Len: 0]
     Sequence number: 0    (relative sequence number)
     Acknowledgment number: 0
     Header Length: 32 bytes
   ▷ Flags: 0x002 (SYN)
     Window size value: 8192
     [Calculated window size: 8192]
   ▷ Checksum: 0x2213 [validation disabled]
     Urgent pointer: 0
   ▷ Options: (12 bytes), Maximum segment size, No-Operation (NOP), Window scale, No-Operation (NOP), No-Operation (NOP), SACK permitted
```

Figure 6.2

Having all of these fields in the protocol header, TCP can provide us with:

- *Data reordering*
- *Data retransmission* in case of packet loss by using **sequence numbers.**
- *Reliable applications*

Each packet (or packet group) has a **sequence number** associated with it. If the recipient receives a certain number of packets (defined by the sequence number), then it will send back an acknowledgment message (ACK) for those (received) packets:

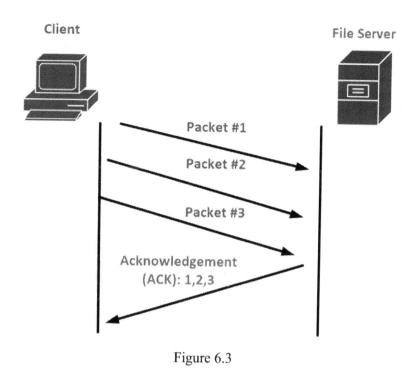

Figure 6.3

Thus, it's easy for the recipient to figure out what packets have reached and what packets need to be retransmitted. If the source (client) does not receive an ACK for any packets, then it will retransmit those packets.

At first, when two devices want to communicate via a client-server connection, a **3-Way Handshake** session must be established.

How does a Client establishes a connection to a Server ? (3-Way Handshake)

As I said earlier, when a server has to communicate with a client, the two will form a connection between them, known as the **3-Way Handshake**. Now, let's take a look of how this handshake takes place:

At first, the client (the one who starts the connection) will send to the server:
1. a synchronisation message (**SYN**) - marking the beginning of a session
2. The server will respond with an acknowledgement (**SYN-ACK**)
3. The client will also respond to the server with an acknowledgement (**ACK**)

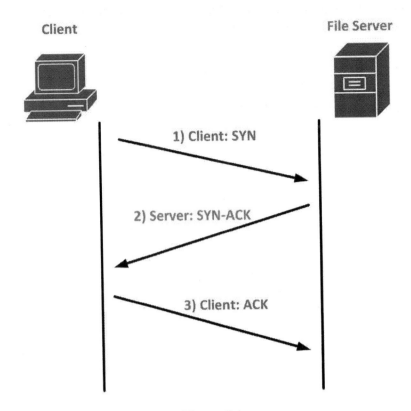

Figure 6.4

Here's a Wireshark capture with the 3 packets shown above:

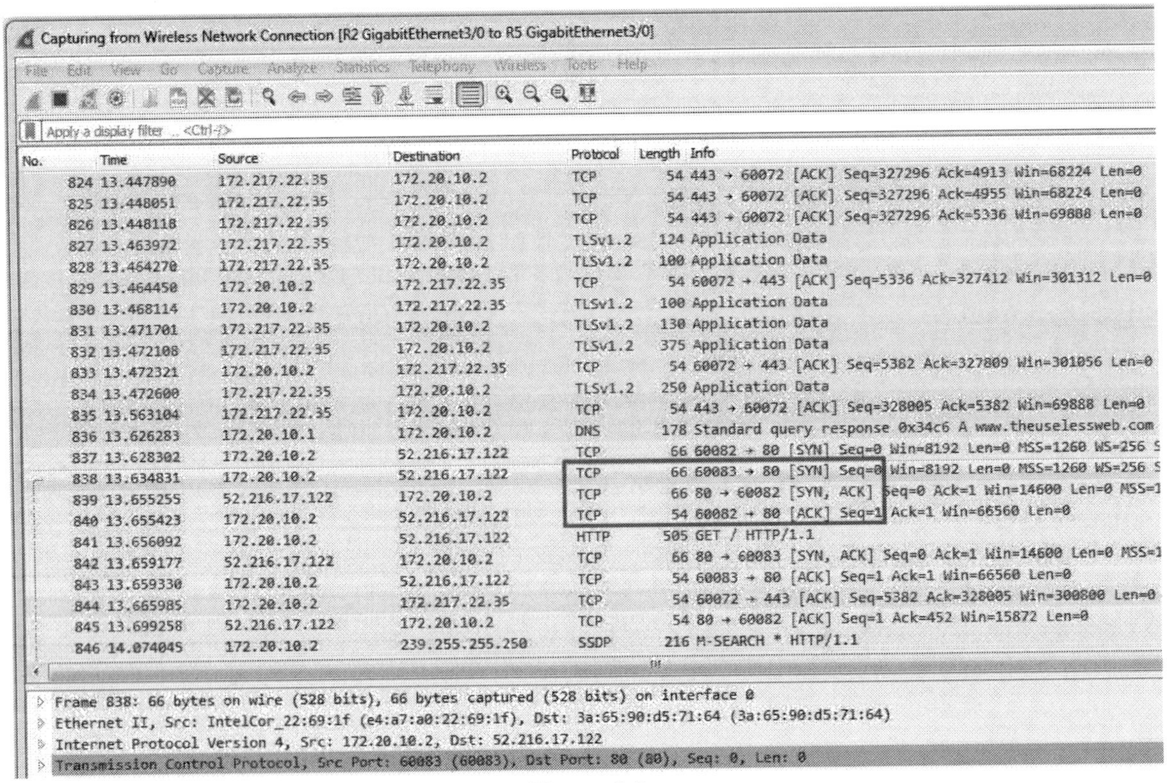

Figure 6.5

This way the **TCP connection** (via **3-way handshake**) between the client and the server was **established**. Now the two devices can communicate (send web traffic, file transfer, etc.).

This mechanism of the 3-way handshake helps ensure the client and the server, that all packets are being counted (sequenced), order and verified at their destination. In case some of the packets are missing they are going to be resent (by the sender).

How does TCP terminates a connection ?

After all packets have been transmitted, the connection must end. This is similar to a 3-way handshake, but this time 4 packets are being sent:

1. **the client** send a **FIN** packet
2. **the server** responds with an acknowledgement (**FIN-ACK**)
3. **the server** also sends a **FIN** message
4. **the client** replies with an acknowledgement, **FIN-ACK**

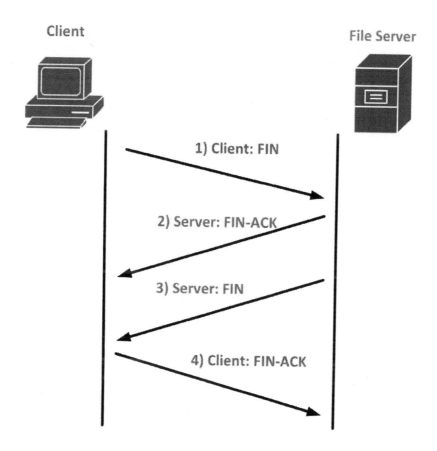

Figure 6.6

Here's the Wireshark capture with the concepts discussed above:

No.	Time	Source	Destination	Protocol	Length	Info
3486	-165.344927	10.92.32.10	10.84.166.102	TCP	1314	[TCP segment of a reassembled PDU]
3487	-165.344829	10.92.32.10	10.84.166.102	TCP	1314	[TCP segment of a reassembled PDU]
3488	-165.344813	10.84.166.102	10.92.32.10	TCP	54	64806 → 80 [ACK] Seq=240 Ack=41154 Win=66560 Len=0
3489	-165.344151	10.92.32.10	10.84.166.102	TCP	1314	[TCP segment of a reassembled PDU]
3490	-165.344117	10.92.32.10	10.84.166.102	TCP	1314	[TCP segment of a reassembled PDU]
3491	-165.343983	10.84.166.102	10.92.32.10	TCP	54	64806 → 80 [ACK] Seq=240 Ack=43674 Win=66560 Len=0
3492	-165.343918	10.92.32.10	10.84.166.102	TCP	1314	[TCP segment of a reassembled PDU]
3493	-165.343905	10.92.32.10	10.84.166.102	TCP	1314	[TCP segment of a reassembled PDU]
3494	-165.343896	10.84.166.102	10.92.32.10	TCP	54	64806 → 80 [ACK] Seq=240 Ack=46194 Win=66560 Len=0
3495	-165.343861	10.92.32.10	10.84.166.102	TCP	1314	[TCP segment of a reassembled PDU]
3496	-165.343780	10.92.32.10	10.84.166.102	TCP	1314	[TCP segment of a reassembled PDU]
3497	-165.343771	10.84.166.102	10.92.32.10	TCP	54	64806 → 80 [ACK] Seq=240 Ack=48714 Win=66560 Len=0
3498	-165.343721	10.92.32.10	10.84.166.102	TCP	1314	[TCP segment of a reassembled PDU]
3499	-165.343708	10.92.32.10	10.84.166.102	TCP	1314	[TCP segment of a reassembled PDU]
3500	-165.343641	10.84.166.102	10.92.32.10	TCP	54	64806 → 80 [ACK] Seq=240 Ack=51234 Win=66560 Len=0
3501	-165.343605	10.92.32.10	10.84.166.102	TCP	1314	[TCP segment of a reassembled PDU]
3502	-165.343592	10.92.32.10	10.84.166.102	TCP	1314	[TCP segment of a reassembled PDU]
3503	-165.343534	10.84.166.102	10.92.32.10	TCP	54	64806 → 80 [ACK] Seq=240 Ack=53754 Win=66560 Len=0
3504	-165.343490	10.92.32.10	10.84.166.102	TCP	1314	[TCP segment of a reassembled PDU]
3505	-165.343478	10.92.32.10	10.84.166.102	HTTP	1011	HTTP/1.1 200 OK (application/x-ns-proxy-autoconfig)
3506	-165.343457	10.84.166.102	10.92.32.10	TCP	54	64806 → 80 [ACK] Seq=240 Ack=55972 Win=66560 Len=0
3507	-165.343257	10.84.166.102	10.92.32.10	TCP	54	64806 → 80 [FIN, ACK] Seq=240 Ack=55972 Win=66560 Len=0
3509	-165.306572	10.92.32.10	10.84.166.102	TCP	60	80 → 64806 [ACK] Seq=5597 2 Ack=241 Win=15744 Len=0
3593	*REF*	10.84.166.102	10.86.35.73	TCP	1314	[TCP segment of a reassembled PDU]

```
[TCP Segment Len: 0]
Sequence number: 240     (relative sequence number)
Acknowledgment number: 55972     (relative ack number)
Header Length: 20 bytes
▷ Flags: 0x011 (FIN, ACK)
```

Figure 6.7

And so the TCP connection between the two devices will end.

2) UDP (User Datagram Protocol)

UDP is the exact opposite of TCP (it doesn't retransmit packets, it doesn't establishes a connection before sending data, it doesn't reorders the packets etc.). **UDP simply sends** the **packets** from a specific **source** to a specific **destination** without being interested of the connection's status. The **advantage** of using this protocol is the **low latency** which allows for the smooth transition of the application with the lowest delay possible.

Thus, UDP is **suitable** for **real-time applications** (eg. Voice, Video traffic) that need to **reach** the **destination as quickly as possible**. In figure 6.8 you can see how the UDP header looks, and compared to TCP, it's much more simpler and efficient in processing and bandwidth utilisation.

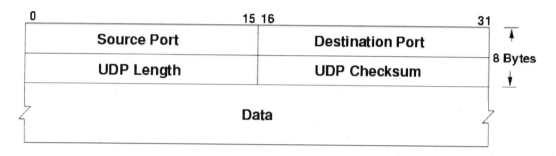

Figure 6.8

Because we were talking about real-time applications such as Skype, Facebook Live, CS Online, here are a few requirements for VoIP (**Voice over IP**) or other similar delay sensitive apps:

* **Delay: < 150 ms:** Open CMD, type ping 8.8.8.8 and see the delay of every packet
* **Packet Loss: < 1%:** 1 second of voice = 50 pkts of 20 ms audio each => 1% of 50 = 0,5;
    (this means that at every 2 seconds we can lose max 1 packet)
* **Jitter (variable delay): < 30ms**

At the beginning of this chapter I told you that TCP uses segments (as the PDU), but in the case of the UDP protocol things change a little bit. **UDP** does not use segments, it uses **datagrams**
(it brakes the data into datagrams which are smaller in size than segments).

In figure 6.9 is an example of a UDP header (datagram). As you can see (compared to figure 6.2) it's much smaller than the TCP header (segment):

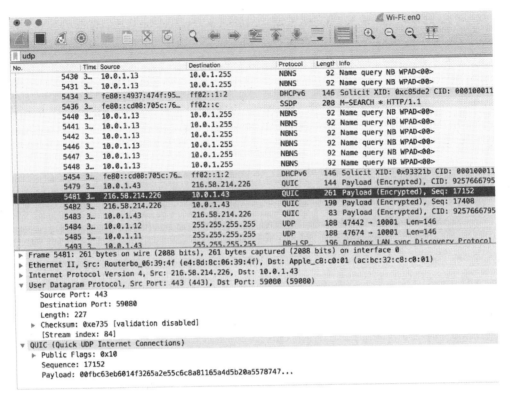

Figure 6.9

In figure 6.9 we can see the UDP protocol in action. This time I selected a protocol called QUIC (Quick UDP Internet Connections) that runs over UDP (as we can see in the figure). It helps us with the **transmission of traffic** in an **encrypted way** (the Payload is Encrypted).

I also want to state the reduced complexity of the UDP header (as seen in Figure 6.8 and 6.9), namely the **source port**, the **destination port** and the total length of the header.

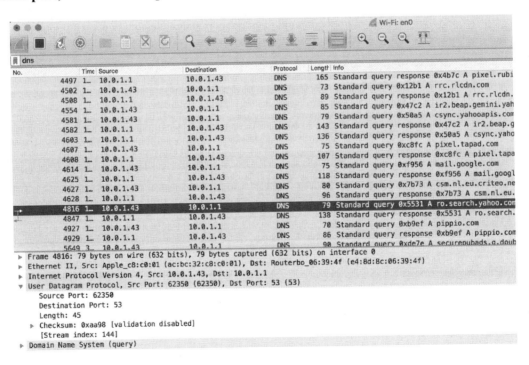

Figure 6.10

52

Now, let's take another example. In figure 6.10 we can see another type of traffic:

- **DNS queries** (name resolution of a domain to an IP address).

We can see that the DNS protocol (which will be discussed in more detail in Chapter 7) uses UDP for data transport, and more specifically uses **port 53.** As you can see I mentioned the term "port". In this case we are not talking about a physical port (the place where you plug the cable in), but we are referring to a **logical port** which identifies the *network applications that are running* on a *device* (be it Router, Server, Laptop etc.).

3) Ports

A **port** uniquely identifies a **network application** (Web server, DNS server, etc.) on a device in a network. Each port has an identifier (a number, ranging from **1** to **65535**). When a PC sends a request (for a web page) to a server, this request will contain (among other) the following information:

Source IP: PC

Destination IP: Server

Source Port: 29813 (randomly generated by the Browser)

Destination Port: 80

In other words: The PC's browser (with a source port of 29813) requests from the server (Destination) a web page (port 80).

Example #1 - TCP ports

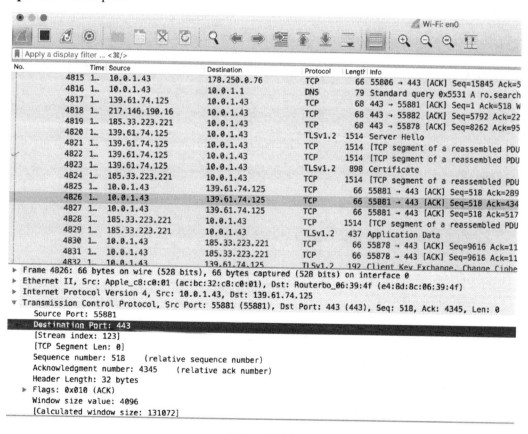

Figure 6.11

53

Now let's take a few examples where we can analyse and talk about what we've been discussing in this chapter.

As you can see in Figure 6.11, there is a communication flow between 2 devices (source: 10.0.1.43, destination: 139.61.74.125).

The **source port** (generated randomly) in this case is 55881 (most likely was generated by a browser - Google Chrome, Safari, Firefox, etc.) and the destination port is **443** (**HTTPS**, a secured web application).

Thus, the source addresses is requesting a web page hosted by a server placed somewhere in the Internet. Besides that, in the lower half of the figure, you can see the structure of the TCP header with all of it's fields that have been shown in figure 6.1.

In this case we can easily identify the ports, the sequence number of the current packet (segment), the acknowledgment number, window size and so on.

Example #2 - UDP ports

Moving forward to the UDP protocol, in figure 6.12 you can see a Wireshark capture:

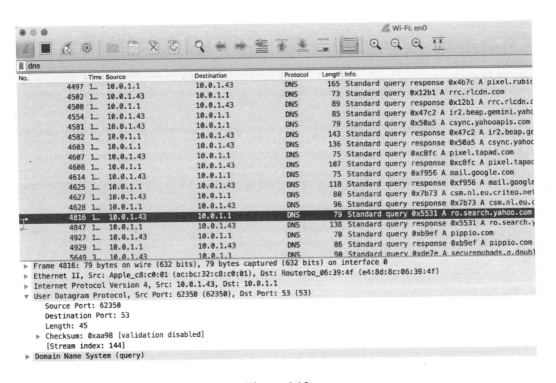

Figure 6.12

In the example from figure 6.12 you can see a process similar to the previous one, but in this case it's the **UDP protocol** (actually DNS [layer 7] which uses the UDP protocol [layer 4]).

Here you can see the **2 ports** (**source** - 62350 and **destination** - 53) of the 2 devices participating in the communication (source: 10.0.1.43 and destination: 10.0.1.1).

One thing that I would like that you remember is the simplicity of the UDP header (figure 6.12) versus the TCP header (figure 6.11). The most important elements in the UDP header are the two ports (source and destination).

Chapter 7 - Layer 5, 6, 7
Session, Presentation, Application

In this chapter we are going to talk about the last 3 layers of the OSI model: **Session, Presentation** and **Application.** Let's get started with the first of the 3.

a) Layer 5 - Session

The purpose of the **Session Layer** is to *create a session, maintain, and terminate it* between 2 network applications. A session (communication) consists of exchanging a request-to-answer data flow between 2 devices connected to the Internet. The device that **requests the data** is know as the **client**, while the device that **provides** the data is know as the **server.**

An important protocol at this layer is Lightweight Directory Access Protocol (**LDAP**), a protocol that manages, searches and modifies a directory service (the place where the **user data** (*usernames, password, other user information*) is stored). With the help of this protocol, we can exchange user key elements in the network (more precisely in the network security process):

- **User authentication**
- **User authorisation**

b) Layer 6 - Presentation

The purpose of the Presentation layer is to "serve data" in a specific format (eg. JSON, JPEG image format, PNG, etc.). At this layer, **data is structured in a certain** form and is delivered to be interpreted by server-based applications.

For example, the data can be in one of the following formats: JSON (Figure 7.1), XML (Figure 7.2), etc.

```
{
    "employees": [
        {
            "id": 52626,
            "name": "Employee One"
        },
        {
            "id": 26565,
            "name": "Employee Two"
        }
    ]
}
```

Figure 7.1

```
<SampleXML>
    <Colors>
        <Color1>White</Color1>
        <Color2>Blue</Color2>
        <Color3>Black</Color3>
        <Color4 Special="Light">Green</Color4>
        <Color5>Red</Color5>
    </Colors>
    <Fruits>
        <Fruits1>Apple</Fruits1>
        <Fruits2>Pineapple</Fruits2>
        <Fruits3>Grapes</Fruits3>
        <Fruits4>Melon</Fruits4>
    </Fruits>
</SampleXML>
```

Figure 7.2

Another example for this layer is **data encryption**. Encrypted data (aka. secured data) is intended to hide the original content in another format. In Figure 7.3, you can see a capture of the encrypted traffic in Wireshark.

```
4 90 A3 31    .$V.sI.. ..^..E...<]..@......D2a^4......W04..1
F 6A 10 10    @...F.%......@.$L.N....U.....&.........B.@0j..
6 D9 33 3C    ..=.+.".P<.&....}........o....T.@P.ni._.#...3<
0 73 75 2E    sl-.w.....E.4$s.`j.xrc4.[y.A.... 0HT..d.a.su.
6 B0 78 D1    (F..T.X....d. ........j.......w.V=.+(h.s.E....x.
7 6B F4 D2    [.n.h!+...HUd]....T.1........,F.BB P.>.n....k..
1 17 55 CA    ....:q6..hK.j.......].2................R.zA.U.
1 D5 00 9C    ..>..5[..E.E..n.....*7.B.g+..]+.`.]..X........
5 FF ED D0    KI.O.H........*.6..`......bE.P_.I.............
9 77 A0 B0    .....5*...8.+o.< w.GvA.V*.zH....g....F<.]..w..
E A3 F1 88    ....+.?wsP7.,..k\.`.....TE..'X{...m.a...s....
C 92 C1 C3    .Z,z..vw^.!....r.Q.mh.C.d..g.GMk...T.X.......
7 10 4E 71    \k..F....]FD....#.9................%....]..Nq
7 23 93 9B    ........I&N...b..[R.9.BC.!.fR.7..{..2V._{:.#..
F DC B9 F0    .....z..<.JP....r@..........~...3.3..S..&......
F 7A 16 27    ...(,~M.........y:....le........N\....k.._z.'
C FE 46 BE    .Wl.u..!o.....5.:LIE..5)+VH....H.^.G.....T..F.
7 18 FD 05    ....2b...FV.E..^..I..3.R.....Q..^`..g}:"f.g...
E B1 CB 2A    v+!..>.].tAp.@........x._..VN..W5....46.H...*
E 11 78 6D    =.L.\.<...8x....!..\.@..Y.3..#)0J..'.=.`E...xm
F 0C 17 CE    .e.Cv..X.X..RQ@.oj.c...hp...b..,{...2.&).. ...
D E7 8D FB    X.1..J.eI.6n.......i....=F...*;Zth.. ..^X.....
1 C0 B0 C1    <......Pq"T!......fyw..<.."...f(z.S...........
E 17 8D BF    ...9...}...4... S.+.\6.......8.V.....7pK.z....
```

Figure 7.3

c) Layer 7 - Application

When talking about applications, in this context, we are strictly referring to **network applications**. These network applications are generally those offered by a server (eg: a web application, email, remote access to a PC, etc.). Here are some protocols that work at this layer:

- **HTTPS** (port 443 TCP)

- **SSH** (port 22 TCP)

- **DHCP** (port 67/68 UDP)

- **DNS** (port 53 UDP)

For example, **HTTPS** (HyperText Transfer Protocol **Secure**) is a protocol that helps us with accessing websites in a secure way. **HTTP** is the unsecured version that only offers the functionality (the ability to access webpages). Bellow in figure 7.4 is an example of the HTTPS protocol:

Figure 7.4

Another important protocol that helps us access the Internet (eg: websites) is **DNS** (**D**omain **N**ame **S**ervices) that transforms a domain name (eg: www.google.com) into an IP address (because all network devices **USE the addresses IP**, not the domain name).

Figure 7.5

In figure 7.5, the IP address of Google.com is **216.58.214.238** and was found by using the **nslookup** command.

Network Applications

Now, let's take a look at a few of these applications. Bellow are a few protocols that are used very often by network applications:

HTTP

- **Description:** used for Web traffic (transports HTML files from server to client)
- **Port:** 80
- **Transport Protocol:** TCP

HTTPS

- **Description:** used for **securing** the Web traffic
- **Port:** 443
- **Transport Protocol:** TCP

FTP

- **Description:** allows the transfer of files between a client and a server
- **Port:** 20/21
- **Transport Protocol:** TCP

DNS

- **Description:** finds the IP address of a domain name (ex: google.com -> 172.217.18.67)
- **Port:** 53
- **Protocol de Transport:** UDP (client), TCP (server)

Telnet
- **Description:** remote access connection with a network device (Router, Switch etc.) or server
- **Port:** 23
- **Transport Protocol:** TCP

SSH

- **Description:** **secured** remote access connection with a network device (Router, Switch) or server
- **Port:** 22
- **Transport Protocol:** TCP

DHCP

- **Description:** dynamically assigns IP addresses (and other info) to all end-device in the network
- **Port:** 67/68
- **Transport Protocol:** UDP

SMTP

- **Description:** mail transfer protocol, used between mail servers
- **Port:** 25
- **Transport Protocol:** TCP

IMAP

- **Description:** protocol for transferring mail from the server to the client (the emails will be stored on the server)
- **Port:** 143
- **Transport Protocol:** TCP

POP3

- **Description:** transfers emails from server to client (and stores them on the client's PC)
- **Port:** 110
- **Transport Protocol:** TCP

RDP

- **Description:** allows you to connect remotely (from the GUI) to a Windows, Linux or MacOS machine
- **Port:** 3389
- **Transport Protocol:** UDP

Now, I let's take a more in depth look at some of the protocols mentioned above:

DHCP

DHCP (**D**ynamic **H**ost **C**onfiguration **P**rotocol) is a network protocol that dynamically provides the following information to the devices connected to the network:

1) IP Address + Mask

2) Default Gateway

3) DNS Server

The **IP address** will help us identify each device in the network while the **network mask** establishes the network range (and size). The **DNS server** helps us **translate the name** (ex: google.com) into an **IP address** (216.58.214.227). All this information is provided by a server (in smaller networks, it's usually the Wireless Router).

How does DHCP work ?

When a **end-device** (PC, smart phone, tablet, smart TV, etc.) **connects** to the network, it will send a Broadcast request (to all network devices) hoping to **find a DHCP server** which can provide him with the information mentioned above. In figure 7.6 you can see the DHCP process happening between a end-device and a DHCP server (Router in this scenario).

1) DHCP Discover

When a DHCP server (in small networks it will generally be a Wi-Fi Router) sees such a message in the network, it will immediately respond with a:

2) DHCP Offer   (which contains the information mentioned above)

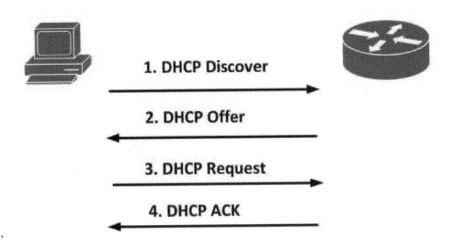

Figure 7.6

Finally, the device (the PC in this case) will agree to the DHCP server's "offer" and will send a request for it:

3) DHCP Request

After the DHCP server receives message #3, it will respond with:

4) DHCP ACK   // as an acknowledgement to the request provided by the device

Configuring an IP address with DHCP on Windows

Now that you saw how DNS works, let's take another example and see how we can assign an IP address via DHCP on Windows XP / 7 / 8.1 / 10. We'll see how we can do this both from CMD and GUI.

1) Assigning an IP address with DHCP from the CMD

The way we can assign an IP address via DHCP in Windows, from CMD, is through the following command: **>ipconfig /renew**

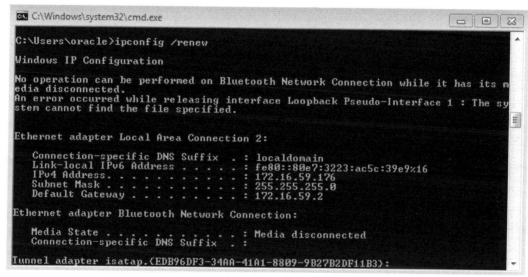

Figure 7.7

The result ? An IP address, a subnet mask and a default gateway. If we want to find out more information (such as DNS, MAC address or even DHCP server) we have the following command:

>ipconfig /all

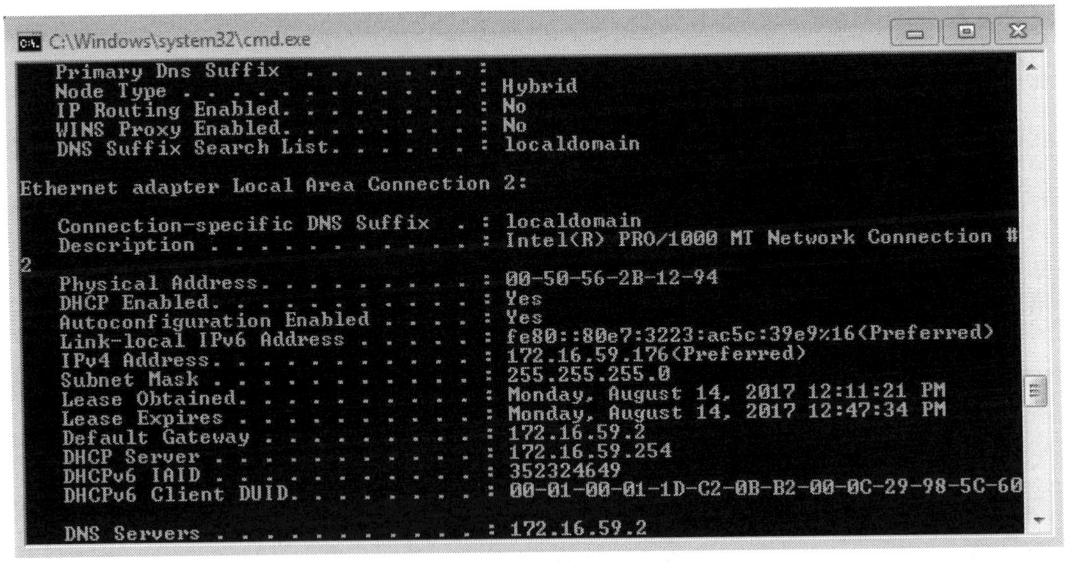

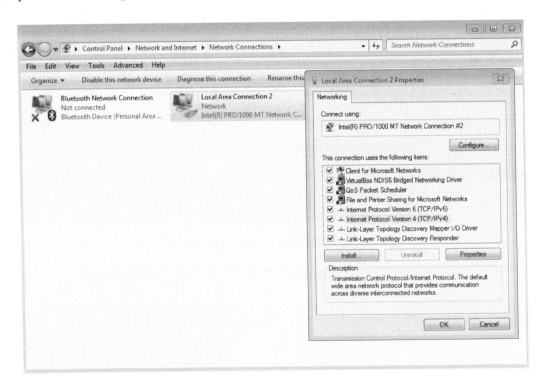

Figure 7.8

2) DHCP from the GUI in Windows

At this point we can set up an IP address:

Figure 7.9

We'll select IPv4 -> **"Properties"** and be at the point from figure 7.10:

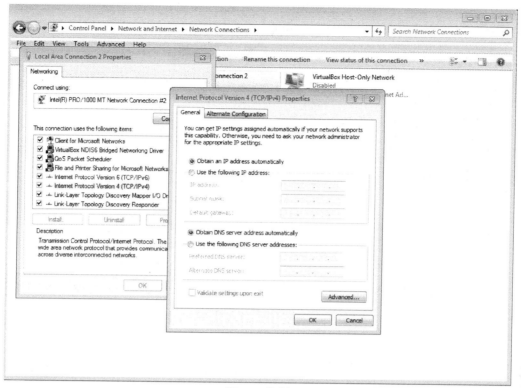

Figure 7.10

Now we'll select **"Obtain an IP address automatically"**, followed by **"Obtain DNS server address automatically"** and then press "**OK**". These two options will tell the PC to send a DHCP request in the network, requesting an IP address (+ the other settings).

2) Telnet

Telnet is a network protocol that allows remote connection to a network device (Router, Switch, Firewall, etc.) or to a server.

It is very widespread being installed on the majority of devices, but it has a **major disadvantage**: the connection is **UNSECURED** ! I mean, all the communication between 2 devices using Telnet is sent in **clear text** and can be easily intercepted by a hacker.

In order to achieve the connectivity, a program that we can use on Windows is PuTTY (figure 7.11). With PuTTY we can connect to a device via Telnet, SSH or even through the console (Serial) via a cable.

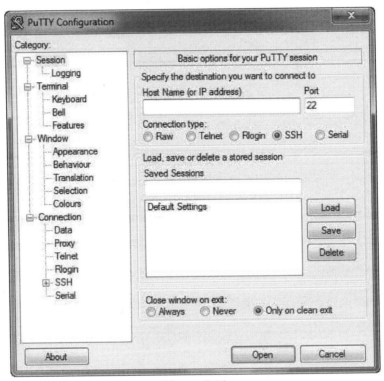

Figure 7.11

Telnet uses **port 23 on TCP** and can be used on Linux, Mac, Windows or any other device. The recommendation is to **not use it** (due to the fact that the **traffic is not encrypted**, only transmitted in clear text).

3) Secure Shell (SSH)

SSH is a protocol that **allows remote connections** to network devices (Router, Switch, Firewall, etc.) or servers (i.e. Linux, Unix, Windows). The **connection** is **SECURED** (all traffic will be encrypted by both parties).

This is **the most widely used** protocol for remote access due to its security and its flexibility which are built in.

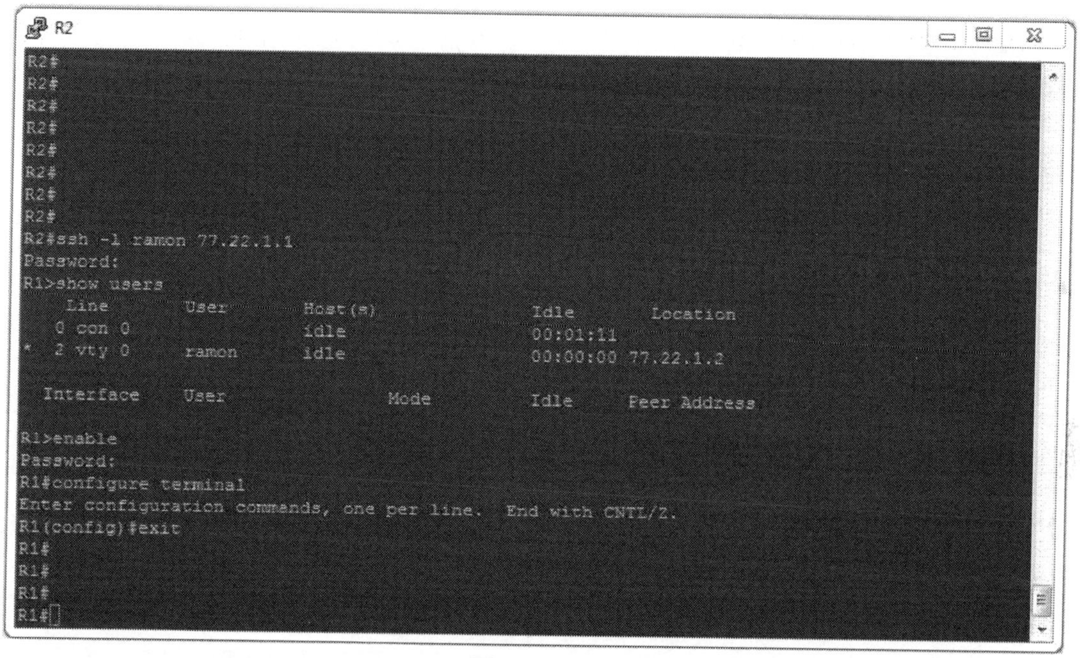

Figure 7.12

SSH uses **port 22 on TCP** and can be used on Linux, Mac, Windows or any other device.

4) RDP - Remote Desktop Protocol

Because we spoke about 2 protocols that allows us to remotely access our network or server devices (through the CLI), let's also take a look at a protocol that gives us the same capabilities of accessing a device remotely, but comes with a graphical user interface (**GUI**). This protocol provides us access to our PC or laptop (Windows).

Here's an example of the RDP protocol, a scenario in which I connected (remotely through the Internet) to my desktop from another location.

Basically (in Windows) we have a window (Figure 7.13) with multiple fields in which we enter the IP address (or the name) of the PC, followed by the login credentials (user + password):

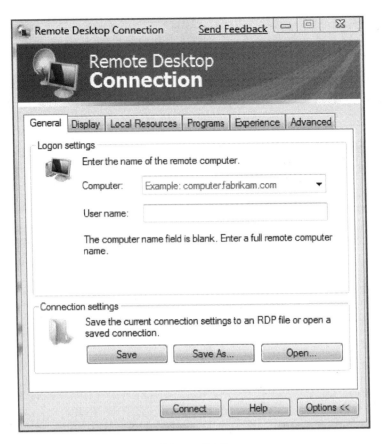

Figure 7.13

And in Figure 7.14 we can see how such a RDP connection looks like (a simple window where we have the desktop of the computer specified earlier).

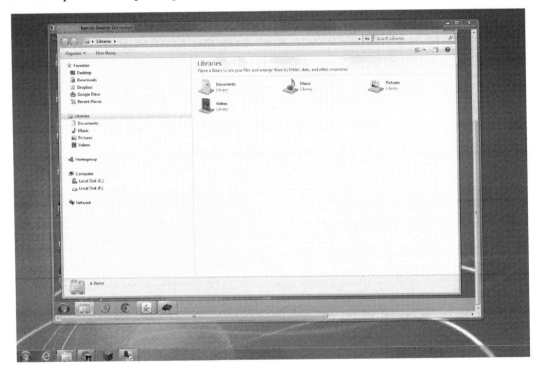

Figure 7.14

Chapter 8 - Cisco IOS & Intro to the CLI

When it comes to Cisco devices (Routers and Switches), they all have one thing in common: the **Cisco IOS. IOS** stands for **I**nternetwork **O**perating **S**ystem and is the "engine" that powers these network devices.

In the following chapter we'll talk mainly about IOS and how can we manage it, but for now I just want to let you know that we have 2 ways of working with it via the CLI or the GUI.

The **CLI** stands for the Command Line Interface and is the way we **configure** all **IOS** devices (we give special commands - from an interface- that will drive a certain behaviour). Thus, we will have **total control and access** of the Routers or Switches.

The **GUI** is the Graphical User Interface and is a much more friendlier way of managing a device. Most often we use it when setting up small network devices such as Home Wireless Routers (Wi-Fi).

In the following section we will see how we can interact with the Cisco IOS (versions **15.2** or **12.4**) through the CLI.

Introduction to the CLI - Basic Router Configurations

In this section we will move to the practical part of this eBook, and we'll start with the **basic configurations** on a Cisco Router.

Also, in this section we are going to use a network simulator (in order to create our network environments) so I highly recommend you download the **Cisco Packet Tracer** version **6.2** (that you can find **HERE**). This program gives us the ability to learn and practice the configuration of networks (PCs, network devices, servers, etc.) without requiring a physical devices.

Here are some of the basic configurations that we'll going to do on our Cisco Router:
- The **name** of the device (Hostname)
- **Passwords** (encrypted or in clear text)
- **IP addresses** on the interfaces
- **Remote access** on the network devices via Telnet or SSH

a) Access Levels

In Cisco IOS we have **3** main **access levels** (for security purpose), where the user can do various things: #1 tests the connectivity (to the Internet) (>) by using commands such as **ping** or **traceroute**; #2 **see** what's actually happening with the device (#); #3 or make any **changes** - **(config)#**.

When you connect to a Cisco device (Router, Switch, Firewall, etc.) you will be in the **user exec mode (>)** - *1st access level*. In this access level (**user exec**) you are **limited** in terms of the commands you can give to the device (generally commands such as ping, traceroute, etc.). In order to move up the ladder and access a higher level of commands and privileges we must enter the following command:

Router>**enable**

Now, we are officially in the 2nd access level, the **privilege mode - R1#**.
Here you can see everything that's happening on the equipment (through various forms of **show** commands), but you **CAN NOT make changes**.

Router>**enable**
Router#
In order to be able to make changes on the device, we must go on a higher (the 3rd and last) access level with even more privileges, known as the **global configuration mode**:

Router#**configure terminal**
Router(**config**)#

Here in this configuration mode, you can make **any changes** you want on any Cisco device. This global configuration mode is equivalent to the Windows **Administrator** or the **root** user on Linux. Here are a few of the commands that I recommend you get familiar with:

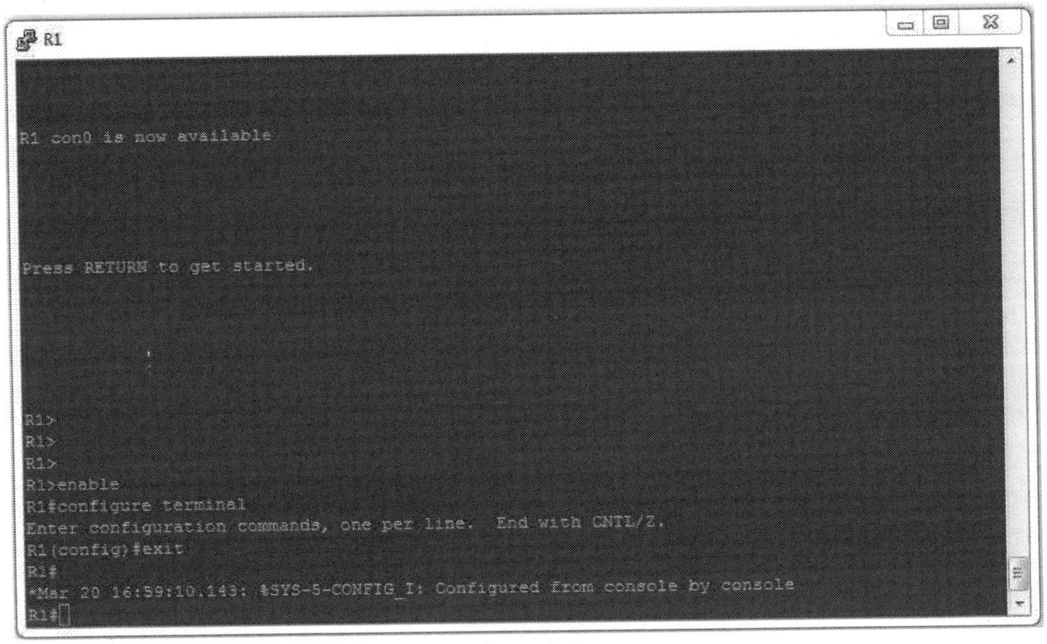

Figure 8.1

If we want to write a longer command (and not feeling like typing it :D) we have a solution that provides us with a faster (and more accurate) way of inserting commands.

If I write the **R1#show run** command, and press the **TAB** key, it will **autocomplete** it. Also "?" Will show us the (next) commands available.

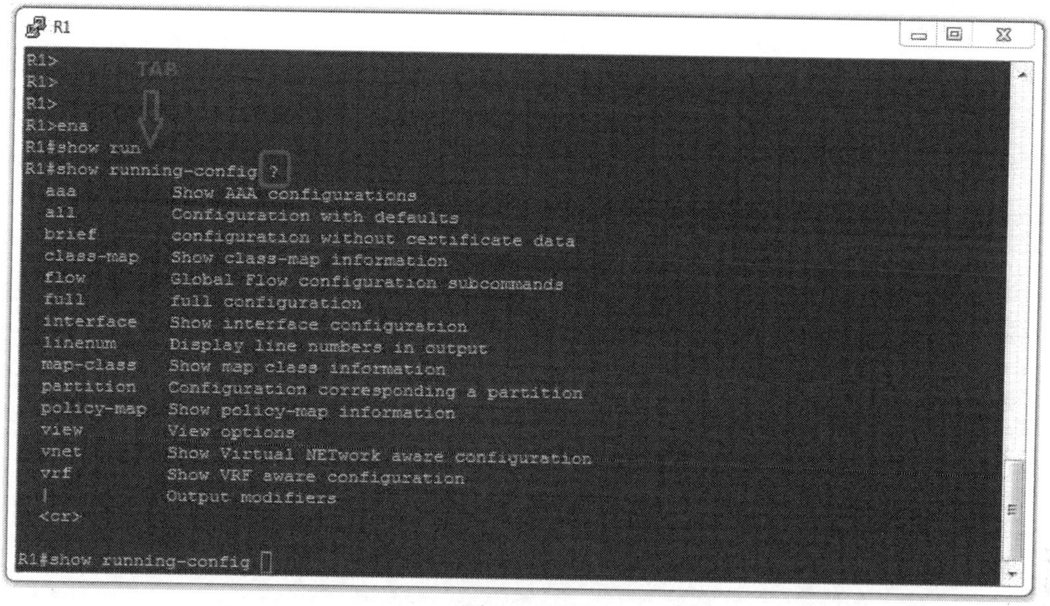

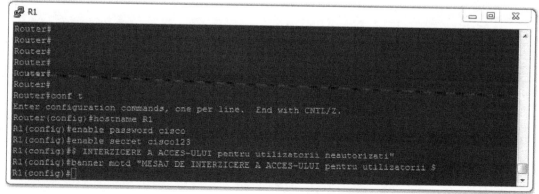

Figure 8.2

b) Setting a device name (Hostname)

In order to change the name of the Router (or the Switch) we can enter the following command:

Router(config)#**hostname** ROUTER_NAME
ROUTER_NAME(config)#
Figure 8.3 illustrates this command and other from the following points.

c) Securing access on the Router

Now let's see how we can secure the access of our Router by setting a password. Here's how we can set a **password** in **privilege mode** (#):

Figure 8.3

Router(config)#**hostname** R1

R1(config)#**enable password** cisco

or

R1(config)#**enable secret** cisco123

The following command will set a warning banner for those that try to login to the device:
R1(config)#**banner motd** "UNAUTHORISED ACCESS DENIED"

Maybe you're wondering what's the difference between the **enable password** and the **enable secret** commands ? Well, here's the difference (figure 8.4):

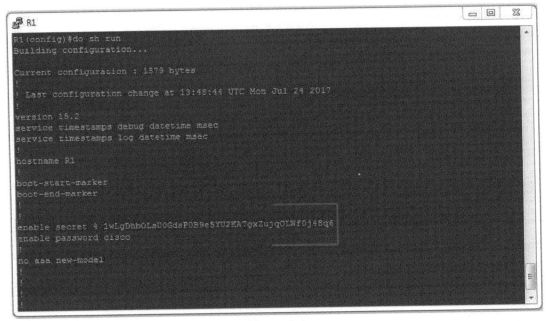

Figure 8.4

As you can see one is stored in an **encrypted format** (#enable secret) and the other is stored in **clear text** (#enable password).

Let's take the following topology and start configuring the Router for network access (reachability):

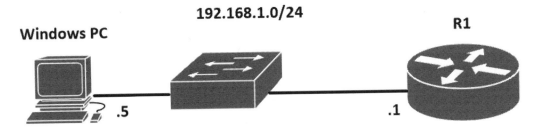

d) Configuring an IP address on the Router

As I said in Chapter 4, a Router **interconnects** multiple networks through **ports** (usually 2 or 3). We are calling **port** a physical place where a cable can be plugged. The other name that we assign to the logical part of a port is **interface**.

So, to sum things up:

- **Port = Physical**
- **Interface = Logical**

For example: "we will set an **IP** (logical) address on an **interface** and **connect** the cable (physically) to a **port**"

These interfaces must have an IP address configured to communicate within the network and the interface must be turned **ON**. In figure 8.5, you can see how we can set an IP address on an interface:

```
R1
R1#
R1#
R1#
R1#conf t
Enter configuration commands, one per line.  End with CNTL/Z.
R1(config)#interface Gi3/0
R1(config-if)#ip address 192.168.1.1 255.255.255.0
R1(config-if)#no shutdown
R1(config-if)#
*Jul 24 13:47:46.979: %LINK-3-UPDOWN: Interface GigabitEthernet3/0, changed state to up
*Jul 24 13:47:47.979: %LINEPROTO-5-UPDOWN: Line protocol on Interface GigabitEthernet3/0, changed state to up
```

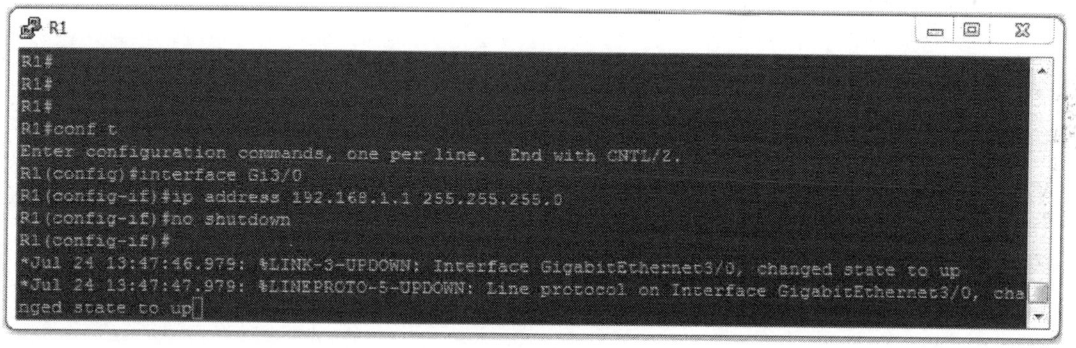

Figure 8.5

R1(config)#**interface** FastEthernet0/0
R1(config-if)#**ip address** 192.168.1.1 255.255.255.0
R1(config-if)#**no shutdown**

f) Configuring remote access on a Router (Telnet, SSH)

A little earlier in chapter 7 we learned about Telnet and SSH, and now it's time to configure them on our Router. So let's move on first with Telnet:

Telnet

Figure 8.6

R1(config)#**line vty** 0 14
R1(config-line)#**password** cisco
R1(config-line)#**login**

At first we want to enter our **virtual lines** (15 in total) ,then set the password (in this case "cisco") and, at the end, start the Telnet process #login.

SSH

As we discussed in chapter 7, SSH is a protocol that ensures remote connection to a LAN or Internet device in a secure way. In order **to configure SSH on a Cisco device** we have to take following steps:

1. Creating a user and password
2. Setting a Domain name
3. Generating a pair of public & private key - for security purpose
4. Enabling the process on the virtual lines (vty) with the command #login local

So, here (in figure 8.7) is the actual config of SSH on a Cisco Router:

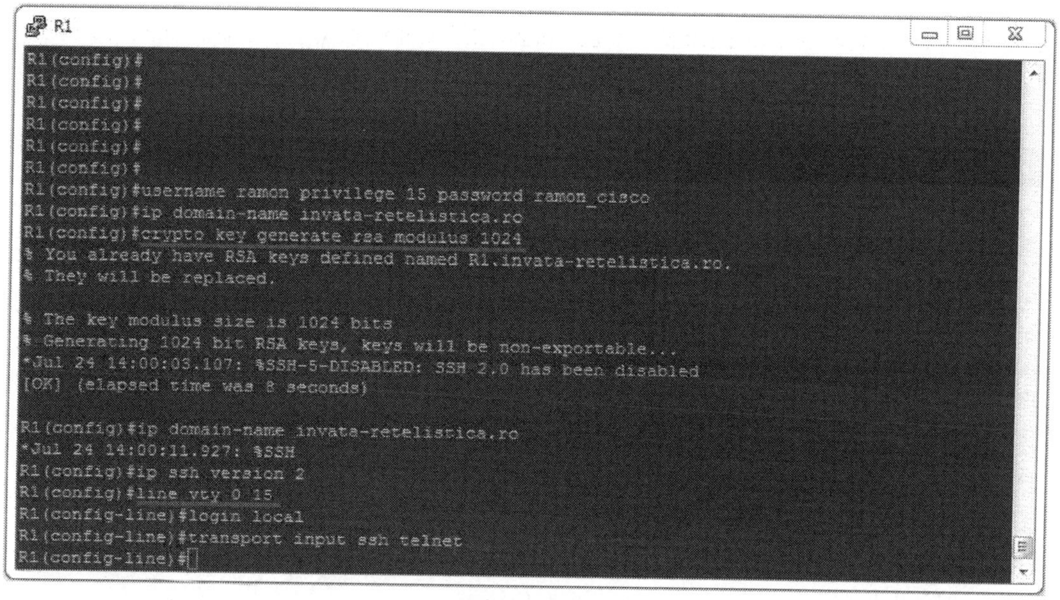

Figure 8.7

R1(config)#**username** admin **privilege** 15 **password** admincisco321

R1(config)#**ip domain-name** my.home.lab
R1(config)#**crypto key generate rsa modulus** 1024
R1(config)#**ip ssh version** 2

R1(config)**line vty** 0 15
R1(config-line)#**login local**
R1(config-line)#**transport input ssh telnet**

Practice

Now it's time to put theory into practice. In this lab we are going to implement the concepts discussed above. Please follow the requirements below and configure the devices accordingly.

PURPOSE: Accommodation with the CLI. Basic configurations on Cisco Routers and Switches. Ensuring end-to-end connectivity

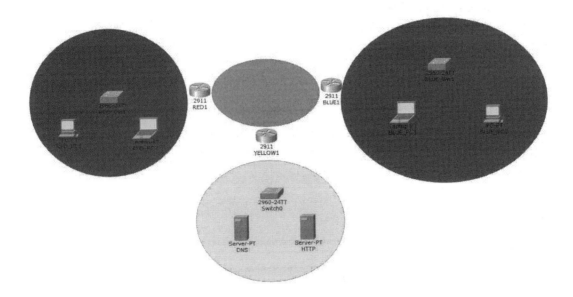

Lab Requirements

0) Wire the equipment properly (pay attention to the types of cables needed)

1) Set IP addresses on Routers, Switches, and PCs

- **RED:(LEFT)** 10.16.22.0/24
- **GREEN**: (MID) 89.12.0.0/24 (subnet this network into smaller ones of sizes no larger than 2 usable addresses)
- **BLUE**: (RIGHT) 192.168.0.64/27
- **YELLOW**: (DOWN) 172.30.33.128/25

Assign the first IP address of the network to the Routers, the following available IP addresses to the PCs and the last IP address to the Switches.

2.1) Set the Hostname and enable password

2.2) Set the following Banners on the Routers:

("ONLY AUTHORIZED ACCESS")

3.1) Configure Telnet on RED1, RED_SW1, BLUE_SW1
- Use the password: secretP@$$

3.2) Configure SSH on BLUE1 and YELLOW1
- Use any username or password you like

4) Ensure end-to-end connectivity between the networks (by using Static Routes)

5) Test the connectivity with the ping command, between:

- PCs within the same network (LAN - RED, BLUE)

- PCs & Routers

- PCs from opposite networks

- PCs and Servers (access their IP addresses from the built-in browser)

Preview of "CCNA Command Guide"

This section is for you, the reader to have a preview of one of my other books.
Click here to check the rest of the "CCNA Command Guide" The Complete CCNA Routing & Switching Command Guide for Passing the CCNA Exam

2) ROUTING

a) IPv4

Configuring Static Routes

```
//static route configuration (destination / mask and next hop Router)
R1(config)#ip route destination_network mask next_hop_IP
```

```
R1(config)#ip route 192.168.10.0 255.255.255.0 77.22.1.2
```

```
//static default route (to the Internet)
R1(config)#ip route 0.0.0.0 0.0.0.0 77.22.1.2
```

Configuring RIPv2

//creates the RIP process

R1(config)#**router rip**

//sets the version of RIP

R1(config-rtr)#**version 2**

//turns off the automatic summarization of RIP routes

R1(config-rtr)#**no auto-summary**

//adds a network (directly connected) in the RIP process

R1(config-rtr)#**network** 10.0.0.0

//sends the default route information to the other Routers in the network

R1(config-rtr)#**default-information originate**

Example:

R2(config)#**router rip**

R2(config-rtr)#**version 2**

R2(config-rtr)#**no auto-summary**

R2(config-rtr)#**network** 192.168.10.0

R2(config-rtr)#**network** 77.22.1.0

R2(config-rtr)#**default-information originate**

R2(config)#**ip route 0.0.0.0 0.0.0.0** 77.22.1.2

Verifying

R1#show ip route

R1#show ip protocols

R1#show run | section [rip | route]

IPv6

//starting the IPv6 process on the Router

R1#ipv6 unicast-routing

Setting an IPv6 Address

R1(config)#**interface** Gig0/1
R1(config-if)#**ipv6 address** 2002:ABCD:1254::1/64

Configuring Static Routes

//static route configuration for IPv6 (destination / mask and next hop Router)
R1(config)#**ipv6 route** destination_network/mask next_hop_IP

R1(config)#**ipv6 route** 2002:ABCD:1234::/64 2002:AAAA::1
R1(config)#**ip route ::/0** 2002:AAAA::1

Configuring RIPng (RIP next generation)

//creating a new RIPng process
R1(config)#**ipv6 router rip** NAME
R1(config-rtr)#**exit**

//enabling RIPng at an interface level
R1(config)#interface Gig0/0
R1(config-if)#**ipv6 rip** NAME **enable**

Example: (starting RIPng on both interfaces of R2)

R2(config)#**ipv6 router rip** RIP_PROC
R2(config-rtr)#interface Gig0/0
R2(config-if)#**ipv6 rip** RIP_PROC **enable**
R2(config-rtr)#interface Gig0/1
R2(config-if)#**ipv6 rip** RIP_PROC **enable**

Verifying

R1#show ipv6 route
R1#show ipv6 interface brief
R1#show ipv6 protocols
R1#show run | section route

Thanks for reading, don't forget to **review this book** and **Click here** to check the rest of the "**CCNA Command Guide**" The Complete CCNA Routing & Switching Command Guide for Passing the CCNA Exam

65811719R00044

Made in the USA
Middletown, DE
04 March 2018